Advance Praise for

Diary of a Compost Hotline Operator

This is a funny, idiosyncratic and enormously informative handbook
on the rites and wrongs of composting. Like any well-wrought compost
heap, it is a collection of materials — in this case, diary entries, recipes
and madcap meanderings — which combine to produce something
both spiritually uplifting and entirely useful.

— DES KENNEDY, author of *Crazy About Gardening*

From Mike the flailing tai chi fanatic to Wes the head gardener
who gets blamed for everything that goes wrong because he has gone
on yet another holiday, Spring Gillard entertains as she informs.
She left me not only with laughter, but with hope that things will
turn out OK as long as there is green in our cities.

— MARY APPELHOF, author of *Worms Eat My Garbage*

I thoroughly enjoyed this book. Spring brings an important message
home. Her ability to tell humorous stories brings the magic of
composting to life. And the underlying educational message within the
stories — along with all of the tips and resources — will open the eyes
of any non-believers, converting them into composters overnight!

— DAVID TARRANT, gardening television host and
author of *A Year in Your Garden*

Spring's diary gives us insight into the profound example of change
that is City Farmer. We get the real dirt on everything from the basic
compost recipe, to examples of the fascinating unpredictability of
gardens (even those tended by experts). Good information.
Easily digested. Each of us can do our bit for the planet.

— MOURA QUAYLE, Dean, University of British Columbia Faculty of
Agricultural Sciences

This book is a *must read* in our office. It has made us look at our work
in a whole new way. Spring's passion for compost and her commitment
to all things green in the city comes through on every page. She invites
us to gather around the compost bin to laugh and learn.

— STEVE FRILLMANN, Executive Director, Green Guerillas, New York

So how much fun can it *be* to get up to speed on compost piles, worms, water conservation and cob houses from an urban gardener's perspective? And on the other hand, how much can you learn about *anything* when you keep breaking up in giggles every third paragraph? A lot, it turns out — an awful lot. And the proof is Spring Gillard's absolutely delightful *Diary*.

— CAROL LEE FLINDERS, author of *At the Root of This Longing* and *Rebalancing the World*

Diary of a Compost Hotline Operator is a practical and creative guide for compost programs. I wish I had been given a copy when I started working in this field ten years ago at Brooklyn Botanic Garden in New York City. Spring Gillard provides a top-notch blueprint for programs in a multitude of settings. Every city's solid waste manager should have one.

— ELLEN KIRBY, President of the American Community Gardening Association and Director of Brooklyn Botanic Garden

This is a delightful manual that's an actual page-turner, because Spring knows how to sneak complex information into the background of some great yarns. Basic do-it-yourself information is what we need to fuel the Power of One that's going to save the planet, and Spring knows how to deliver it. — Rot on!

— WAYNE ROBERTS, coordinator, Toronto Food Policy Council, and author of *Real Food For A Change*

Spring Gillard's 'edible essays' are edible indeed — very inspirational, informative and full of spicy humor. Such writing is so needed these days to counter the unsustainable globalization and monoculturing of our planet.

— DAN JASON, author of *The Whole Organic Food Book*

Diary of a Compost Hotline Operator

EDIBLE ESSAYS ON CITY FARMING

Spring Gillard

NEW SOCIETY PUBLISHERS

Cataloguing in Publication Data:
A catalog record for this publication is available from the National Library of Canada.

Cover design by Diane McIntosh. Composter image © Norseman Plastics. Trowel image ©Artville.
Printed in Canada by Friesens Inc.

New Society Publishers acknowledges the support of the Government of Canada through the Book Publishing Industry Development Program (BPIDP) for our publishing activities.

Paperback ISBN: 0-86571-492-4

To order directly from the publishers, please add $4.50 shipping to the price of the first copy, and $1.00 for each additional copy (plus GST in Canada). Send check or money order to:

New Society Publishers
P.O. Box 189, Gabriola Island, BC V0R 1X0, Canada
1-800-567-6772

New Society Publishers' mission is to publish books that contribute in funda-mental ways to building an ecologically sustainable and just society, and to do so with the least possible impact on the environment, in a manner that models this vision. We are committed to doing this not just through education, but through action. We are acting on our commitment to the world's remaining ancient forests by phasing out our paper supply from ancient forests worldwide. This book is one step towards ending global deforestation and climate change. It is printed on acid-free paper that is **100% old growth forest-free** (100% post-consumer recycled), processed chlorine free, and printed with vegetable based, low VOC inks. For fur-ther information, or to browse our full list of books and purchase securely, visit our website at: www.newsociety.com
NEW SOCIETY PUBLISHERS   www.newsociety.com

For Wally and Wanda,
your love and laughter
keep me afloat

Contents

My whole life has been spent waiting for an epiphany,
a manifestation of God's presence, the kind of
transcendent, magical experience that lets you see
your place in the big picture. And that is what I had
with my first compost heap.

BETTE MIDLER
Los Angeles Times
May 8, 1996

25 YEARS OF CITY FARMING, 1978–2003

IN 1978, A GROUP OF YOUNG ENVIRONMENTALISTS working at the Vancouver Energy Conservation Center stumbled across a book called *The City People's Book of Raising Food* by William and Helga Olkowski. It described in everyday language how the authors grew all their own food right in the middle of the city of Berkeley. This inspiring book led us on an exploration of urban food production, which continues today, twenty-five years later.

Working at an energy center, the first thing that struck us was the amount of fossil fuel used to transport food from far away farms to our supermarkets. We quickly realized that there were real savings for people who grew food at home. Such a simple act struck us as revolutionary, especially when we saw that there were other environmental and social problems that could be addressed as well. The urban farmer became our new-found hero!

For someone like myself, who grew up cutting the lawn with a push mower, edging it with a shovel, and digging out dandelions by hand, urban farming was a revelation — by pulling back a carpet of grass and planting a vegetable seed, I could put food on the table.

Bob Woodsworth, a founding member of the group, took us to his grandmother's house to see her tidy steaming compost and then drove us to see the garden of a family friend who cultivated fruit and vegetables in his very large yard. Bob's philosophy of making change in society through information sharing rather than aggressive confrontation became one of our main strategies.

On a stroll down the back lanes of Chinatown, we marveled at an elderly Asian woman planting bok choy and growing water vegetables in an old bathtub with claw feet. A few blocks over an Italian immigrant grew figs and bay leaves and kept chickens. These mentors were all old people and our sixties' generation philosophy of "don't trust anyone over 30" was given quite a jolt.

Every garden was a surprise, and our interest in all things to do with farming in the city grew. What exactly were organic fertilizers and were they really safer than synthetic ones? Would car exhaust affect the crops we planted next to a busy street? And how could we change those ancient anti-livestock by-laws?

Sitting in a small co-op bakery, we reinvented ourselves by starting a non-profit society named, City Farmer — Canada's Office of Urban Agriculture. The first part of the name was a catchy, easy-to-remember moniker, the latter part expressed the serious side of our work — feeding people, social justice, and environmental awareness. We joked that the bureaucrats in Ottawa might mistake us for an official government department and send us funds, but that never happened. However, I was once introduced as "Canada's Unofficial Minister of Urban Agriculture."

Eager to get the word out, we put together an eight-page newspaper using the skills we had learned working on university papers — typesetting articles, pasting them onto layout sheets of cardboard, and shipping them off to a printer. We loved writing the stories and seeing our names in print, but the arduous task of mailing out and delivering 2,000 copies of the paper was more than we'd bargained for.

Although most people loved the idea of producing food in the city, we were surprised to see opposition. Our first story, titled "Chickens in Soup," was about a woman fighting city hall to keep a few hens in her back yard. One alderman was outspoken in his attack, saying that allowing livestock inside the city was like "going back to the dark ages." His vision of a modern city included skyscrapers, lawns, and asphalt — a place far removed from the farm where so many of our Canadian ancestors grew up. The divide between the country and city was large.

It was just that divide that City Farmer wanted to end. While many of our generation dreamed of going back to the land in some idyllic rural setting, we chose to bring that image of country to the city — in miniature if you like — in our gardens. We were hooked on the metropolitan lifestyle of museums, theaters, and a multitude of ethnic restaurants, and wanted to add another fashion to the urban mix, both laid-back and productive — something that could recycle our wastes, help cleanse the air and soil, and keep us healthy.

Our newspaper was just the beginning of our efforts to promote urban agriculture. In 1979 we invited the California guru of small-scale food gardening to town and put him on national radio. John Jeavons, the author of (a mouthful of a title for a book), *How to Grow More Vegetables, Fruits, Nuts, Berries, Grains, and Other Crops Than You Ever Thought Possible On Less Land Than You Can Imagine*, received a huge and immediate response from his interview on the Canadian Broadcasting Company. Letters and requests for information poured in from across the country. Seeing the reach of the larger media made a strong impression on our tiny organization and we added another tenet to our list of strategies — create interesting stories and share them with the press.

By 1981 we were eager to get out of the office and get our hands black with soil rather than ink, so we created a demonstration food garden on a parking lot behind a new environmental center. Lead by head gardener Catherine Shapiro, volunteers used a jackhammer to open the back yard hardpan, which soon turned into a lush organic plot. Our urban Eden showed the public what a garden looked like in every season. Reading about gardening was one thing, but seeing seedlings planted, finding a pest under a cabbage leaf, tasting blueberries picked fresh from the bush, and uncovering sweet kale in winter was a transformative experience.

And so we added another strategy to our wisdom list — start demonstration projects and get hands-on experience so that we know what we're talking about. Over the next decade we undertook several major urban agriculture experiments.

Close to where we lived in Chinatown was a large empty field. Using a year-long federal grant which paid for an organizer, we were able to help a group of interested community members get a lease from the city's Parks Board for use of the three-acre piece of land to start a garden. Today, Strathcona Community Garden is the most written about allotment garden in Canada and is a destination point for thousands of tourists.

Dr. Gary Pennington, a University of British Columbia education professor, asked us to be part of his project to transform the asphalt school yard of his old elementary school (Lord Roberts) into a model "green" playground. City Farmer put in the food garden and hired instructors to show the kids and teachers how to grow food right in their school yard. One grade seven girl was shocked to learn that we'd spent $200 on a truck-load of smelly manure which she thought could be better spent on a couple of attractive outfits for herself. The highlight for the kids was making a salad for their teachers using their own garden produce. The director of nutrition for the province was so impressed with the project that she organized a garden contest to judge the best school garden in all of British Columbia.

But how could we involve the elderly, the sick, and the disabled in urban agriculture? Volunteers built a small "ability garden" in our demonstration garden using raised planters, which gave access to people in wheelchairs. We then put a tiny job announcement in the newspaper to find staff (the fewer words, the cheaper) — "must love gardening, must love people." The response was overwhelming and three big-hearted "horticulture activity coordinators" were hired to take care of visitors.

Local care facilities were thrilled to have a fresh air destination and brought disabled children from a local hospital, 100-year-old residents from seniors' homes, and the sick from care centers. Kids who couldn't use their arms or legs were fed fresh-picked strawberries and ice cream, old people plucked flower petals to decorate their hats, and the more agile visitors in wheelchairs leaned into the raised beds and delighted in getting their hands in the soil. The day concluded with a civilized after-noon tea under the shade of our large cherry tree.

In 1990, the provincial government began a program urging citizens to cut the amount of waste they send to landfills — and suddenly composting was recognized as a useful technology for everyone, not just organic gardeners. The staff of the solid-waste department for the city of Vancouver and the regional govern-ment asked us to use our teaching garden to promote back yard and worm composting which we were happy to do because mak-ing rich soil is the foundation of urban agriculture. Spring Gillard joined head gardener Wes Barrett as the compost hotline opera-tor and they became the Compost Duo.

At the same time that a local performance artist was being chased out of town for planning to crush a rat named Sniffy between two canvases, we introduced a rodent-resistant compost bin to prevent rats from dining out on compost piles. The bin, which was designed with both a top and a bottom and no holes larger than one-half inch, was adopted by cities across North America.

The new sustainable city involves more than just having a job and being a good consumer. It demands that we become resource conservers, protectors of the environment, and pro-ducers of food. One of our early mentors summed up his economic reason for planting a food garden by reminding us that people pay taxes on both back and front yards as well as the house they live in, so why not make the vacant land pay for itself in food?

New hats are added to our teaching garden every year as we show residents what they can do to help solve urban problems. Technologies such as rain barrels to collect water for the garden, composting toilets to save thousands of liters of water used by flush toilets, and mulching lawn mowers to help cut yard waste trucked to the landfill are demonstrated at the site. But perhaps the biggest change in our work has taken place away from the garden soil in a mysterious part of the environment named cyberspace.

In 1994, City Farmer went on-line, publishing "Urban Agriculture Notes" — the descendant of our paper tabloid. The World Wide Web was in its infancy but already the promise of what was to come was clear. New countries connected to the Internet weekly, faster than anyone expected, and people from around the world discovered that they could read reports, share stories, and put questions to an audience whose size they'd never dreamed of before. In barely ten years, that promise has proved truer than we expected and the virtual world is part of the day-to-day life of millions of people. It is perhaps no coincidence that the concept of urban agriculture has been accepted so quickly.

The City Farmer website is visited by hundreds of thousands of people — four million hits in 2002, 186 countries visiting. But more telling than these indicators is the "site visibility." According to Marketleap.com, Cityfarmer.org ranks in the same category as Coke.com — a brand name known around the world which spends millions on advertising. The Web has leveled the playing field and allowed tiny groups, who do not have the huge resources available to corporations and governments, to place their product in front of people.

Because of the Internet, our back yard now includes the global community. City Farmer's work involves traveling virtually via the computer from country to country documenting, communicating, and networking. This is a long way from delivering a few thin newspapers to corner stores.

In 1999, City Farmer was honored to be made a partner in the Netherlands-based Resource Center on Urban Agriculture and Forestry (RUAF). Funded for five years to "facilitate the integration of Urban Agriculture into the policies and programs of national and local governments and international funding agencies" the RUAF has already set up regional focal points in Africa, the Middle East, South America, and Asia.

Twenty-five years ago we could barely find a single reference to the term "urban agriculture". Today, whether it's at the United Nations' Food and Agriculture Organization in Rome or at the World Summit on Sustainable Development held in Johannesburg, development specialists are talking about city farming as a strategy to address rapid urbanization and growing poverty.

It has been said that the easiest way to predict the future is to invent it. Already, we have begun to generate the next twenty-five years of our work. We recently hired a market research company to poll residents and found that 44% of people in Greater Vancouver households produce some of their own food. That research built on another project in progress. In an attempt to better document the urban agriculture potential within metropolitan areas, we purchased the latest aerial photos of the city and, using Geographic Information Systems software, discovered that one third of the total area of a typical residential block is landscaped and has the potential for food growing. City Farmer staffers are always dreaming up exciting new projects like these ones, which they then turn into reality. The seeds of our future are being planted daily in our tiny greenhouse office next to the garden.

Spring Gillard spends most of her time in that bright greenhouse — greeting visitors, providing well-researched answers to callers on the Hotline, and concocting new projects that are usually guaranteed to get us some media attention or at least give us a few laughs. As you may guess, we laugh a lot at City Farmer. Spring once coerced a few of us into writing a script proposal on worm composting for an episode of Seinfeld, the TV show. We mailed it to the producer's office in a plastic worm bin complete with newspaper bedding and jelly worms. Jerry never got back to us.

Spring's previous years in advertising help her translate her passionate interest in environmental issues into stories that capture the public's imagination. Whether you're laughing at the antics of us silly farmers or learning something interesting about cob sheds, *Diary of a Compost Hotline Operator* will give you a taste of life at City Farmer. And as you read this wonderful, humorous book, you will also come to know our delight in serving the public, the pleasure we take in sharing important research, and the pure enjoyment we get in poking fun at ourselves.

MICHAEL LEVENSTON
Executive Director
City Farmer — Canada's Office of Urban Agriculture
June 2003

INTRODUCTION: FULL CIRCLE

I REMEMBER SITTING ON MY GRANDMOTHER'S STEPS, salt shaker in hand, eating a big, sun-warmed tomato fresh from the garden. Nothing ever tasted so good. My grandmother always had a big food garden and she shared its bounty with her large family and her neighbors. My grandpa grew delicious sweet Concord grapes and made wine from them; I had a few potent experiences with his wine when I was in my teens.

My mother was an avid food gardener, too. In my late high school years we lived on a five-acre orchard in the Okanagan Valley. Not only did Mom work side by side with my Dad in the orchard, but she also cultivated a large food garden. She was always out there weeding, hoeing, and harvesting. Then she'd can, pickle, and bake, filling our home with the wondrous scent of motherly love.

Despite these maternal role models, I hated gardening, probably because Mom was always trying to get us to work in the garden with her. My brothers had to manage the irrigation in the orchard and help with the fruit picking, but I usually managed to worm my way out of working. I would occasionally pick the raspberries, but only because Mom would promise me one of her raspberry rhubarb pies. No, I had no interest in gardening — in fact, I went out of my way to avoid it for years and wound up in advertising! The essay entitled *Garden Heart* tells the whole story of how I made the incredible journey from advertising copywriter to compost hotline operator at City Farmer, a non-profit urban-agriculture group in Vancouver, Canada.

I have worked at City Farmer's compost demonstration garden since the spring of 1991. In our beautiful organic garden which is open to the public year round, you will find composters, worm bins, rain barrels, irrigation systems, a sump, a compost toilet, and a cob garden shed amid the food and flowers. Depending on the time of year you visit, you may run into Mike Levenston, executive director of City Farmer, or Sharon Slack, our head gardener. You might even meet Wes Barrett, our former head gardener, popping in over the lunch hour, or at least his effigy, Wet Coast Wes, the scarecrow. You'll get to know the rest of the lovable and eccentric City Farmer characters as you read on.

In addition to answering hotline calls, entertaining visitors and media, we also give wormshops, composting instruction, organic food gardening courses, bugshops, and grass classes. We conduct tours with local and international guests and research various urban agriculture topics for publication in our monthly Compost Hotline News and on our website. Our work extends beyond the garden gates via the Internet as well as through our own travels. Occasionally we accept invitations to speak at garden-related conferences in Canada and the U.S. and we visit urban-agriculture projects and community gardens in other parts of the world. You'll read about my adventures in Cuba and New York City in the last chapter.

It's not just the staff that make up our garden, of course. It's the many wonderful volunteers, friends, suppliers and supporters, the hotline callers, the visitors (both local and international), our fabulous neighbors and their pets (yes, even you, Bootsy). There are the community gardeners, the other environmental groups we share the building with, the compost demonstration gardens in our network — all of them make up our little garden community and they all have tales to tell. People come and go here but they all throw something new onto the compost heap and we are transformed.

I have always learned best through story and I've always liked to tell stories. I also love to laugh and we do a lot of laughing at City Farmer. Nevertheless, we are environmentalists and underneath all our joking and laughing, we take our work very seriously. We do believe that if everyone looked after their own back yard, the world would be a very different place. But we've found that people will digest information better and we will have a better chance of shifting "unsustainable" behavior if we give them a bit of fun while they're learning. For example, our adult wormshops are just an adaptation of our kids' wormshops. They're very hands on and the program is a huge success. It's been running non-stop since 1995 and we fill every class. People leave laughing and are genuinely excited about their new pet worms!

In some circles, urban agriculture is called political horticulture. I'll admit I was attracted to City Farmer not only by the beautiful garden, but also by their Gandhian approach to activism. These City Farmers were not the "tie yourself to the railway tracks" types: they preferred to lead by example and to offer solutions. But for me, growing your own tomatoes in a pot or having a worm bin on your balcony is a political act, as much a symbol of independence as Gandhi's spinning wheel. Growing our own food allows us to feed ourselves and take back some measure of control over what we put into our bodies.

For about five years, in tandem with my garden job, I moonlighted as a video producer/film maker and tried unsuccessfully to get several documentaries and TV series on the garden off the ground. Still, the research and creativity required for those proposals fueled a lot of articles that were subsequently published in newspapers and magazines.

Diary of a Compost Hotline Operator began in 1996 on the City Farmer website (www.cityfarmer.org) as a series of diary entries which chronicled the day-to-day happenings at our small urban food garden. A few years later, I wed the diary entries with the newspaper and magazine articles I had written to create this collection of humorous essays on city farming. As you follow the antics of the crazy cast of characters at the City Farmer garden, I hope you will also learn something about composting, natural lawn care, food gardening, and of course, lust and love in the garden. If you haven't already got your own garden, maybe you will be inspired to plant one. There is a lot of information packed in and around the essays, and lists of contacts and resources to get you started or to enhance what you already know.

I guess my seasonal name should have been a big clue as to where I'd wind up. Funny how we have to travel so far to come back to where we belong. I always tell visitors that the garden shows the complete cycle of life, from seed to earth to tabletop to earth and round again. My life came full circle the day I walked into this garden and if they ever want to get rid of me, they'll have to compost me.

Spring Gillard
Vancouver, BC
June 2003

CHAPTER 1

The City Farmer Compost Rap

April 5

Rats!

Early morning. Isabelle "the Sweet" has run out to the garden to check on the compost bins. I hear a gasp from her as I take my post on the hotline and don my headset. I glance out the greenhouse door and see her standing in front of the west coast cedar bin, a sturdy little, rodent-resistant, wood and wire number (the bin, not Isabelle).

"Don't tell me," I yell out, fearing the little mice munchkins have been at it again.

"Okay," she chirps and turns back to the bin. She's French Canadian and sometimes takes me too literally.

"No, I mean, what is it, mice?" I try again.

"No, I think it's a rat," she says slowly.

I venture slowly into the garden. There in the middle of the pathway, dead as a doornail, plump and glassy *eyed, is a giant, squishy rat. We know it is squishy because Isabelle has stepped on it accidentally. Another casualty of Boots the cat. I stick a pail over top of the rodent offender to hide it from our visitors until our leader, Michael "the Brave," arrives. The long tail (the rat's, not Mike's) sticks out from underneath.*

When Mike finally shows up, he is perturbed. "We haven't had a rat in here since 1990," he says.

"He was probably just passing through, on his way to the neighbor's smelly bin," I console him.

If there's no head gardener around, then blame it on the neighbors, I always say.

On the Compost Crisis Line

"I've just dumped a box of laundry detergent into my compost bin," the man said frantically. "I just couldn't take it anymore. My bin was a fly-infested bog," he gasped. "I had to mud wrestle with flies every time I mixed the thing. My wife was threatening to take it away from me. Can you help me?"

I'm the compost hotline operator at City Farmer's Compost Demonstration Garden in Vancouver, Canada. We teach people about composting and growing food in the city. Every day I talk people through their compost crises from my tiny greenhouse office. Oh, you may think "crisis" is an exaggeration, but believe me, the people who call me are distraught. It's my job to diagnose the problem and cure whatever ails. In virtually every case, the crisis can be resolved with our tried and true Calm-post Recipe.

Like many of my callers, this gentleman had been adding too much green material and not enough brown. So once again I divulged The Recipe:

Alternate two to four inch (5–10 cm) layers of green (grass, garden waste, and food waste) and brown (dry fall leaves, straw, or stripped-up newspaper). Cover food layers with a light sprinkling of soil to suppress smells and flies. Cap off with a brown layer. Mix it all up once every couple of weeks with a pitch fork or compost aerator. Harvest the finished compost in two to three months. But mark my words, if you muck with the recipe, expect trouble to bubble up.

"It was the kind with the phosphates, you know. Lemon-scented," he said remorsefully. "I thought that would kill off the flies. There's gazillions of them."

Perhaps, but what the star of this little soap opera didn't know is that it would probably kill off other microbial life, make his garden soil toxic, and maybe even cause his vegetables to taste soapy.

That's not the first time we've had someone try to make a unique contribution to their compost bin. With over 4,000 visitors a year to our urban food garden and as many calls on the hotline, we've compiled quite a list of unusual ingredients. Here are just a few of the non-compostable items: futons, incense, corks, rubber bands, cigarette butts, ex-husbands. (If it's not obvious why you shouldn't compost these items, please go immediately to www.cityfarmer.org.) And just when you think you've heard it all, you get another call.

"Hello. I have maggots in my composter," he breathed heavily into the phone.

"Maggots?" I said. "Have you been putting meat in your bin?" Big pause.

Sigh. I wish I could punch in a recorded message at this point. A list of the foods you can and can't stuff into your compost bin. A rhyming ditty — no, maybe a rap would be more satisfying:

"No meat, no fish, no po-ohl-tree,
no grains, no fats, they're too smell-y.
Just greens and browns alter-nate-ly,
plus egg shells, tea bags, and caw-aw-fee."

"Did you put some meat in recently, sir?" I snapped out of my de-composition.

GIANT PAUSE.

"Well, I did put a dead pigeon in there last week."

Not that I haven't wanted to compost the pigeons currently cooing and pooing on my apartment balcony but...

"This is a compost bin, sir, not a pet cemetery. Now, I'm going to give you a recipe, a vegetarian recipe. You'll have to fish the pigeon out. No, sir, fish aren't vegetables, either."

I was sitting in my beautiful greenhouse office. The morning light was soft, the air still cool through the open door. In the garden, sparrows flitted in and out of the birdbath, then alit on the tasseled tops of the amaranth. I heard the squeals of children over in the worm corner; one of our school wormshops was in progress. A couple of visitors were chatting with the gardener over by the rain barrels. All was calm, all was right in this urban oasis. And then the phone rang.

"Hello," I said. But all I could hear was heavy breathing. Oh, no, not another one. Well, actually, this caller seemed to be gasping.

"Breathe into a bag," I screamed down the phone line.

"A rat jumped out of my bin just like a Jack in the Box," said the hyperventilating woman. She gulped out her story. She has a bird feeder in the yard that generously drops grain all over the ground (a rat delicacy). Her compost bin backs onto a lovely, dense blackberry thicket (all the better to tunnel from, my dear). She often leaves her dog's food dish outside (a midnight rat snack). Finally, she was dumping only food waste into the bin without covering it with a brown layer (if they can smell it, they'll find it). She might as well have sent out invitations to Jack and his rat pack.

I repeated the recipe slowly, hypnotically, until her breathing returned to normal. Then I presented her with the *piéce de rodent resistance:*

Stop feeding the bin until you manage the rat population (seek professional help at www.cityfarmer.org). For wood bins, line the sides, bottom, and underside of the lid with 16- or 20-gauge wire mesh: half-inch (1.25

cm) will keep rats out; quarter-inch (.63 cm) will keep mice out. Set a sheet of hardware cloth under plastic composters to keep rodents from burrowing up. Then follow the Calm-post Recipe.

I hung up, heartened that another wayward composter had been brought back into balance.

One warm summer day I was on my lunch break, taking a siesta in the garden hammock under the cherry tree. Suddenly I felt a cool breeze on my face. I opened one eye to see a sprightly woman fanning me with a small packet.

"Can I put old yeast into my compost bin?" she asked.

"Hmmm," I said dreamily. "Well, it could make your whole bin rise, and you'd probably have to punch it down and knead it instead of mixing. But hey, you may have discovered a whole new compost activator."

I urged her to try it and report back to us. "There's nothing like the smell of fresh baked compost," I mumbled.

"I'll drop off a couple of my best loaves next time I come by," she chuckled as she skipped through the garden gate.

As I drifted off once again, swaying in the summer breeze, I was grateful for the lull in calls and visits. A quiet lull. Hmmm, a lullaby. A compost lullaby. That's what we need, a song to unrattle the rattled and soothe the sorry. I began to compose it:

"Rock-a-bye baby, makin' compost,
when you add green, make sure you add brown.
When you add food waste, cover it well.
That way your bin will never smell."

Hot Recipes

CITY FARMER'S COMPOST RECIPE:
WET AND DRY, BROWN AND GREEN

STEP ONE

In a rodent resistant bin, create a base of three to four inches (7.5–10 cm) of woody, brushy material to promote aeration (do not mix into pile).

STEP TWO

Alternate layers of green and brown materials; keep the layers two to four inches (5–10 cm) deep. Common green (nitrogen) and wet materials are grass, food scraps (uncooked fruit and vegetables, coffee grounds, filters, tea bags, and eggshells), and garden trimmings. Common brown (carbon) and dry materials are fall leaves, straw, and newspaper strips. Chop up larger materials for faster decomposition.

STEP THREE

Whenever you add a food scrap layer, make sure you sprinkle it with soil and then cap off with a brown layer to prevent smells and flies.

STEP FOUR

Mix bin contents often (a minimum of once every two weeks). This introduces air and gets bin heating up again. Mix older materials with newer materials for faster decomposition.

STEP FIVE

Moisture content of bin should be like a wrung out dishrag. Only add water if pile is very dry after mixing.

STEP SIX

Pile will shrink. Continue to add and mix until bin is almost full. This next bit is optional: place carpet on surface of pile to retain heat and moisture.

STEP SEVEN

Compost is generally ready to use when it looks like humus (after about two to three months). However, aging the compost for another one to two months is recommended.

NO FLIES ON US

If you've been plagued by flies in your compost bin, try this recipe. In a small dish, mix two drops of dish soap and two drops of vinegar with 1/3 cup (83.3 ml) of fruit juice. We set the dish into one of our compost bins and it worked like a charm. In other words, there were a lot of dead compost flies in the dish! It should work for worm bins, too.

Hot Calls

THE PLY-ABLE PROFESSOR

Q: Can I use sawdust from plywood in my compost bin?

A: Doug Kilburn, professor emeritus in the Microbiology Department at the University of British Columbia, says that the glue used in plywood contains phenol-formaldehyde, a very toxic substance, so the sawdust from plywood should not be used.

A REAL CORKER

Q: Can I put corks in my compost bin?

A: True cork is made from the outer bark of oak trees from the Mediterranean region. In small quantities and broken up, the material would break down, as does any wood material. These natural or untreated corks come in one piece and are found in expensive wines. However, most corks are made up of tiny bits of treated oak and held together by food-grade epoxy resin. It's non-toxic, but even so all corks, including the natural ones, may be bleached with chlorine or sulfur dioxide. Residual traces of these materials have been found in home-brewed wine; they leave a wet-cardboard smell and basically ruin the wine. Corks are also hydrophobic(!), so they would act as water repellents in the bin. Our recommendation? Use your extra corks to make a corkboard or cut down on the wine.

April Fool's Day

Flies in the Face of Adversity

A man popped into the garden the other day. I saw him hovering near the Earth Machine, the plastic compost bin offered by the city for $25.

"Can I help you?" I ask.

"Well, I thought maybe you could," he says. "I came down here to find out how to get rid of the flies in my bin, but I see yours are worse than mine."

I glance down at the bin and notice little white mothflies (Psychodidae) escaping from the side air vents. I nonchalantly lift the lid only to temporarily disappear in a cloud of them. As I pick the little offenders out of my nose and off my tongue, I shrug and blame it on Wes, our head gardener, who's on holidays as usual.

Worm Power

"Worms make great pets. They're quiet and all they do is eat and reproduce. In fact, they eat their own body weight in food waste every day. Worms are a wonderful symbol of the power of one."

So begins a class in vermicomposting (composting with worms) at City Farmer's Compost Demonstration Garden in Vancouver, Canada. Instructor Ellen York is in full costume: her long black T-shirt reads *Black Gold and the Power of One;* her worm earrings undulate creepily from her lobes as she belts out the "Compost Rap" to surprised participants.

Apartment dwellers in Vancouver have been taking advantage of this subsidized city program since 1995. After a one-hour mandatory "wormshop," graduates take home a bin, worms, and all the vermi-nalia they need to start a balcony worm farm — all this for Can$ 25. With worms selling for about $40 a pound, it's a steal of a deal. The end product is a dark, nutrient-rich fertilizer for your flowers and garden. Gardeners in the know have been scooping up this expensive "black gold" (a fancy name for worm poo) off nursery shelves for years.

"In the Greater Vancouver Regional District (GVRD), we produce over two million tons of garbage annually— that's enough to fill B.C. Place Stadium twice — all ten acres (four hectares) under the dome," says York. "Just by recycling, you can cut your garbage down by a third. By adding composting into the mix, you can cut it down by another third."

Diversion of organic waste from worm composting makes up a small percentage of the above figure, but municipal solid-waste departments, keen on getting their 3Rs' message out, are hopping on the worm wagon anyway.

"Worms capture people's attention," says Al Lynch, head of the North Shore Recycling Program which takes care of the recycling for three municipalities. "One article on worms in the local paper generates more calls to us than a whole series on back yard composting. Those calls give us opportunities for more education."

In addition to municipal programs for apartments, many schools in Canada and the U.S. are putting worm bins in classrooms. City Farmer has found homes for more than 4,000 bins in classrooms and apartments in the last decade. In Ontario, an estimated 20,000 worm bins have been distributed to apartment dwellers through provincial/municipal programs. In Oakland, California, over 400 worm bins and training kits were distributed to classrooms through Lites, a program dedicated to improving science teaching in elementary classrooms. The VermiLab Program of the department of environmental protection in Montgomery County, Maryland, reaches approximately 10,000 students annually.

Even office buildings are getting into the act. At the British Columbia Institute of Technology in Burnaby, scraps from the cafeteria are composted in large wooden worm bins in the parking lot. And in Nova Scotia, a large-scale worm composting system has been set up on the Greenwood air force base, complete with air temperature control and hydraulic harvesting capabilities.

Worms are a great hook for the media, too. Red wigglers have been featured in national daily newspapers, in magazines such as *Time* and *Canadian Living*, and on national television shows such as *Canadian Gardener* with host David Tarrant. Trade papers such as *Worm Digest* and *Casting Call* serve up news from around the worm world, including scathing reports on get-rich-quick scams and reviews of reputable commercial vermiculture books. It would appear that wormania is sweeping the nation.

The worm movement began in the 1970s with a woman named Mary Appelhof, a biologist from Kalamazoo, Michigan. She wrote the industry bible, *Worms Eat My Garbage* in 1982. Now a highly sought after speaker at science and environmental conferences, Mary has spread the worm word around the world, touring Australia, the Philippines, England, France, Ireland, and Russia.

So could you just go and dig up a bunch of these worms from your garden instead of forking out the 40 bucks? No. Wrong kind of worm. While your garden variety worm is a burrower, traveling deep into the earth, aerating your soil, and subsisting on dirt, the compost worm or red wiggler is a surface dweller, at home in leaf piles, manure piles, and back yard compost bins. If you'd rather not pick through a pile of horse dung, City Farmer maintains a list of worm farmers across North America on their website; you can mail order from most of them.

Meanwhile, back at the wormshop, Ellen York is getting philosophical.

"In this day and age, it's easy to get overwhelmed. We say, 'Oh, there's so much wrong with the world, what can one person do?' At City Farmer we like to say that if everyone looked after their own back yard, the world would be a very different place. Worms are a wonderful symbol of the power of one. "

Worms are not only found in apartment blocks and schoolrooms; they're also at work in cold climate dwellings. Once the back yard compost bin freezes up, many avid composters move indoors and begin feeding their food waste to a worm bin under their kitchen sink, in the basement, or in a heated garage. In Michigan where temperatures can drop to -10°C (15°F), Appelhof surrounds her outdoor worm bench with bales of straw and inserts a birdbath water heater in a two-gallon (eight-liter) container of water to keep her worms toasty. Seven-watt nightlights will also boost temperatures, although the light may inhibit worm activity. Even on the balmy west coast, worm bins should be insulated for the winter — generally a well-padded cardboard box covered in plastic is sufficient.

And just in case you were thinking of keeping your worms atop your stereo speakers or next to the washer/dryer, think again. Worms are vibration-sensitive and you could set off something called worm crawl. While it's unlikely they'll be all over your kitchen floor in the morning, they will amass on the inside of the lid. This is wormspeak for "we are very unhappy."

Another potential problem indoors is leachate spillage. Leachate is a lovely by-product of worm composting. It's a mixture of the liquid from the food waste and the worm castings (again, worm poo!). It makes a highly-concentrated liquid fertilizer — but you need to dilute it at least ten to one before you water your plants with it. If you spill this precious stuff on your carpet, you will never get it out, so handle with care. York uses a turkey baster to suck up the "gravy" every couple of months, and then stores it in a lidded jar.

So just how much of your "garbage" will worms eat? Well, in a 14-gallon (53-liter) bin, you can expect to compost about one gallon (four liters) a week (think ice cream pail). That may not be big enough, especially if you're a vegetarian. Many people start with one bin; then after their first harvest (separating the worms from their castings and remaking the bin), they divide their worms and start a second bin.

And what do worms like to eat? Uncooked fruit and vegetable waste along with coffee grounds and filters, tea bags (remove the little staple, it's hard on their delicate digestion), and egg shells. Grains and cooked food aren't recommended, as they really smell when they break down and can attract rodents or really piss off your neighbors. Meat, fish, dairy, oils, and pickled things are all no no's, too.

"Some people get very creative when it comes to their worms," says York. "We've had people make worm bin coffee tables. Can you imagine the conversations they have when guests drop by?" Another graduate named her pets "the Supremes" and swears they sing Motown when she leaves her apartment!

Hot Recipes

HOW TO SET UP A WORM BIN

So how do you start a worm bin if there are no nice neat kits available in your city? A visit to the City Farmer website (www.cityfarmer.org) will tell you exactly how to set up a bin and where to get the worms, but here are the basics. Start with a plastic storage container, approximately 14 gallons (53 liters) in size. Drill some holes in the sides at the top, and a few in the bottom for drainage. Fill the bin with stripped-up, dampened newspaper and dry, fall leaves or straw; sprinkle in a couple handfuls of dirt; bury approximately one gallon (four liters) of food waste in a corner, and you're ready for the worms — a half pound (224 grams) will do. You'll also want to elevate the bin and put a drip tray underneath to catch the leachate.

DIRT 'N WORMS RECIPE

This is a fun recipe to take to a potluck!

> 2 packages (7 oz/200 gm) of chocolate wafers
> 1/2 cup (125 ml) butter
> 1 package (7 oz/200 gm) of cream cheese
> 2 boxes (5 oz/153 gm) instant vanilla pudding
> 3 1/2 cups (800 ml) milk
> 2 cups (500 ml) whip cream (use the prepared stuff if you like)
> 10 –12 gummi worms (optional)
> 1 clean flower pot (8 inches/20 cm in diameter, 5–7 inches/12–17 cm deep)
> A small assortment of plastic or fresh flowers

Take the chocolate wafers and put them in a plastic re-sealable bag. Smash them to smithereens or until they look like soil. Set aside. Whip the cream (if you are using fresh), and set in fridge. In a large bowl, beat together butter and cream cheese. Add the pudding mix. Gradually mix in milk. Then very carefully (because it gets rather full), add the whipped cream (or pre-fab stuff).

Take the flower pot and alternate layers of the pudding mixture and the cookies, starting with the cookies. If you like, you can also stick the gummi worms in the layers. Once your pot is full, stick the flowers in. If they're fresh, wrap the stems in plastic wrap first. Store in refrigerator.

Hot Calls

LUNG POWER

Q: Do worms have lungs?

A: We asked Mary Appelhof this one. "No. They exchange respiratory gases through their moist skin. Lungs require a musculature system attached to bones to contract and expand the cavity so that air is forced into the vacuum created as the lungs expand. Then muscles contract, forcing air out. Of course, gas exchange takes place on the moist membranes much in the same way that it does on the worm's moist body."

WORM SEX

Q: How long do worms stay together when they're having sex?

A: Mary has videotaped nightcrawlers mating for over one hour, but she wasn't sure about other species.

November 3

Worm Connoisseurs

A woman called the hotline wondering how she should go about "decanting" her worm bin. Naturally, we inquired about the vintage before responding.

Garden Heart

> Compost has an almost mystical quality...Nothing dies as such. All living things complete their cycle and return to the pool of life. There is neither beginning nor end, only the inexorable turning of the great wheel: growth, decay, death and rebirth.
>
> — WILLIAM LONGGOOD
> *A Gardener's Bouquet of Quotations*

I could hardly believe my eyes. A sign had just jumped into my path. The Vancouver Compost Demonstration Garden. I had lived in this neighborhood off and on for years, walked by this very spot hundreds of times and had never noticed this urban garden tucked in behind a row of old houses. But what's so remarkable about my arriving at this garden gate? How did my life lead me down this particular garden path?

I had just arrived back to springtime in Vancouver, B.C., after two and a half years in "Winterpeg," Manitoba, where you snowshoe to work until May. I had run screaming from the world of advertising. No more selling hamburgers and beer for me; my mind had begun to turn to greener fields. I was recycling everything in sight, but so far my only gardening knowledge was contained in pots of pansies on my balcony.

Right before I left Winnipeg, I went to see the movie *Green Card*, a romantic comedy set in New York City. Bronte (Andie MacDowell) is a horticulturist who volunteers with the Green Guerrillas, a group that gifts gardens to inner city communities. She has her eye on an apartment with a greenhouse. But there's one hitch; she has to be married to get the apartment. Enter Georges (Gerard Depardieu), an illegal alien who needs a wife to get his green card. They agree to a marriage of convenience. As they strike their accord, a green chord resounds deep within me.

So there I was back on the west coast, jobless and homeless, sleeping on a friend's floor, still resonating with this movie. I had no idea what I was going to do with my life, so I took to aimless wandering. One day in a bookstore, I picked up a magazine I'd never read before called *The Utne Reader*. And what's the first article I open to? "Zen, Wheelbarrows, and Collard Greens." The author, Dan Barker from Portland, Oregon, gave away gardens just like Bronte did in the movie. It's real, I thought. Maybe I could do something like that.

The very next day I was wandering up a street I had walked many times before, when suddenly the sign jumped into my path: The Vancouver Compost Demonstration Garden. I turned my head to look down the driveway and through outstretched gates, I saw an April garden, bursting with color and new life, wild with scent and possibility. Like a Buddhist chant, the green chord hummed within me, and the chord became a cord, drawing me in. Spellbound, I passed through the gate and stepped into my new life.

A man stood there as if waiting for me. Without greeting him, I said, "What goes on here?"

Michael Levenston, director of City Farmer (as he turned out to be), was unruffled by my stupor and explained the purpose of their garden. "We're here to teach people about composting. We use the organic garden to demonstrate how to grow food in small urban spaces without chemical fertilizers and pesticides. Visitors can see the complete cycle of life here from table top to compost heap and back to earth again."

"Yes, this is where I belong," I said. "Where do I start?"

He pointed me to the head gardener, who signed me on as a volunteer.

I started the next day. And my first job? Sifting worms! Separating them from their castings in the shaded "worm corner." Yes me, an associate creative director, with worm poop under my manicured nails! I never left. The garden healed, soothed, and nurtured me through that warm summer and guided me through a great transition in my life. My life was transformed by this meeting with the earth.

Soon I was teaching "wormshops" to kids and getting paid. Then I was offered a position as Compost Hotline Operator and my office — in the greenhouse! When I wasn't helping people through their compost crises, I was weeding and tending flower beds, or talking to the media about worms, and finally writing about urban agriculture. It seemed that along with the apple cores and banana peels, my skills were being composted, too.

I was not the first to be recycled by this garden. Many preceded me, our head gardener among them. Wes was a French teacher for 25 years before he stumbled in, in search of new life.

Many more followed; burnt-out and soul-starved like me with that telltale look of wonder on their faces. With hands in the dirt, they each go about quietly transforming themselves and eventually return to the world renewed. But they never really leave. This ever-widening circle of city farmers has become a community with the garden at its heart.

As I write this from my sunny little greenhouse office, crocus and primroses are poking their noses out of the chilly soil, and I find myself on the brink of another great transition. Spring's cycle is about to begin anew, but with its rebirth another season dies. My longtime co-worker, Wes, is leaving the garden, moving on to the next phase of his life. He is salt of the earth, our Wes; his presence has kept us all grounded. Like an old married couple we have tended this garden — raking leaves in the fall; making Christmas baskets each winter with fir boughs collected from forest paths; harvesting fresh produce come summer for a local hospice. In among the seed catalogues, rainy day crossword puzzles, and shared lunches, friendship flourished. My heart aches at his departure and I wonder if I will make it through this transition. Is my season here ending, too? I am not sure, but I do know this: no matter where the path leads me, the garden will always be in my heart.

July 10

Sleeping Beauty

Mike caught a young woman sleeping in the garden early this morning. This is not the first time we've had campers here. Our building houses a lot of environmental groups and they have visitors coming in from all over the world to help with their protests. We've had laundry airing on our fence, people peeing on the tayberries, and knapsacks all over the coastal strawberries in the water-wise garden, so this was *not that unusual. But when Mike explained why she wasn't allowed to sleep in the garden (because it's city property, blah, blah, blah), she said ever so sweetly, "Why? Don't the flowers sleep in the garden?"*

She's got you there, Mikey. The California poppies never wake up before 10 a.m.

Contacts and Resources

COMPOSTING

Many cities offer subsidized compost bins now. Check with your local government; try solid-waste, recycling, or utilities departments. If there is no program, you can usually buy compost bins at hardware and gardening stores. They are also available on-line; check out the websites below.

Groups/Organizations

The Composting Council of Canada
16 Northumberland St.
Toronto, ON M6H 1P7
Phone: (416) 535-0240 Fax: (416) 536-9892
E-mail: ccc@compost.org
Website: <www.compost.org>
The CCC sells the Alberta curriculum guide and has a wonderful plant-a-row program.

Seattle Public Utilities
Natural Soil Building Program
700 5th Avenue
Key Tower, Suite 4900
Seattle, WA 98104
Phone: 206-684-4684 Fax: 206-684-8529
E-mail: carl.woestwin@.seattle.gov

Website: <www.ci.seattle.wa.us/util/composting>
For questions about Seattle Public Utilities' back yard
composting program design and operation, visit the
above website.

Seattle Tilth
Natural Lawn and Garden Hotline
4649 Sunnyside Ave. N, #1
Seattle, WA 98103
Hotline: (206) 633-0224 Fax: (206) 633-0450
E-mail: lawn&gardenhotline@seattletilth.org
Website: <www.seattletilth.org>

U.S. Composting Council
4250 Veterans Memorial Highway
Suite 275
Holbrook, NY 11788
Phone: (631) 737-4931 Fax: (631) 737-4939
E-mail: admin@compostingcouncil.org
Website: <www.compostingcouncil.org>

Vancouver Compost Demonstration Garden
2150 Maple Street
Vancouver, BC V6J 3T3
Compost Hotline: (604) 736-2250
Website: <www.cityfarmer.org>

Books/ Magazines/Publications

*Alberta Curriculum Guide: Composting Goes
to School.*
Call the Compost Council of Canada to order:
(416) 535-0240 or e-mail: ccc@compost.org.

Biocycle Magazine.
An excellent monthly trade magazine, available from
419 State Avenue, Emmaus, PA 18049. Phone: (610)
967-4135. <www.jgpress.com/biocycle.htm >
Composting: The Organic Natural Way, by Dick Kitto.

Thorsons Publishing Group, 1988

Let It Rot, by Stu Campbell. Storey Communications, 1990

The Real Dirt, by Mark Cullen and Lorraine Johnson. Penguin Books, 1992

The Rodale Guide to Composting, by Jerry Minnich, Marjorie Hunt, and the editors of *Organic Gardening* magazine. Rodale Press, 1979

Websites

Composters.com. <www.composters.com> They sell bins, too, including the Earth Machine, and have a great selection, colored pictures, and detailed specifications. They also sell vermicomposters and accessories such as aerators and pet-waste digesters.

Compost Resource Page. <www.oldgrowth.org/compost> Includes everything from commercial composters and related industries to poetry. There is also a composting forum on site.

Earth Machine. <www.norsemanplastics.com> This composter is manufactured by Norseman Plastics. Visit this website to find out if there's a s ubsidized compost bin program in your area. Norseman also sells the Wingdigger, a handy compost aerator.

The Greater Vancouver Regional District: <www.gvrd.bc.ca> The GVRD has a number of composting brochures in PDF format on their website. Check out *Here's the Dirt, A Guide to Worm Composting* and their list of compost demonstration gardens in the GVRD.

Another forum site: <www.mastercomposter.com>

WORM COMPOSTING

To register for a City of Vancouver wormshop, call the compost hotline at (604) 736-2250 (Vancouver residents only). Seattle Tilth and the San Francisco League of Urban Gardeners (SLUG) also offer worm programs. Check with your local botanical garden or city solid-waste/recycling department to see if there is a program in your area. By subscribing to some of the newsletters below, you will be plugged in to the worm community at large.

Groups/Organizations

Mary Appelhof
Flowerfield Enterprises
10332 Shaver Road
Kalamazoo, MI 49024
Phone: (269) 327-0108
E-mail: mary@wormwoman.com >
Website: <www.wormwoman.com>
Visit Mary's website for more information on her books, curriculum guides, videos, worm kits, and other wormanalia.

San Francisco League of Urban Gardeners (SLUG)
2088 Oakdale Avenue (off Industrial)
San Francisco, CA 94124
Phone: (415) 285-7584 (285-SLUG) Fax: (415) 285-7586
Rotline: (415) 285-7585
E-mail: info@slug-sf.org
Website: <www.slug-sf.org>
This group has many wonderful urban garden programs including worm composting and some inspiring youth projects. They also have a quarterly newsletter called Urban Gardener.

Vermico
P.O. Box 2334
Grants Pass, OR 97628
Phone: (541) 476-9626 Fax: (541) 476-4555

E-mail: vermico@vermico.com
Website: <www.vermico.com>
They sell worms and other worm equipment as well as
a great business book: *Commercial Vermiculture: How
to Build a Thriving Business in Redworms* and a bi-
monthly newsletter called *Casting Call.*

Worms @ Home Composting Supplies
Phone: (604) 462-9150
E-mail: wormsathome@telus.net
Website: <www.wormsathome.com>
This is the company that supplies our worm compost-
ing program in the city of Vancouver. In addition to
worm bin kits and worms, they have other educational
materials and offer workshops.

Books/Magazines/Publications

Compost by Gosh! by Michelle Portman. Flower Press, 2002

*The Worm Cafe: Mid-Scale Vermicomposting of
Lunchroom Wastes,* by Binet Payne. Flower Press, 1999

Worms Eat My Garbage, by Mary Appelhof. Second
Edition. Flower Press, 1997

*Worms Eat Our Garbage: Classroom Activities for a
Better Environment,* by Mary Appelhof, Mary Frances
Fenton, and Barbara Loss Harris. Flower Press, 1993

Worm Digest. A quarterly trade newspaper out of
Eugene, Oregon. Call for subscription info,
phone/fax: (541) 485-0456 or visit their website at
<www.wormdigest.org>

WormEzine. News and information from Mary
Appelhof about vermicomposting, worms, and other
critters that live in the soil. To subscribe call (269)
327-0108 or visit her website at
<www.wormwoman.com/acatalog/wormezine.html>

Videos/CDs

Worm Bin Creatures, Alive Through a Microscope,
[videotape]. 1998. Produced and narrated by Warren
Hatch, distributed by Flowerfield Enterprises.
Phone: (269) 327-0108 Fax: (269) 327-7009.

Wormania, [videotape]. 1995. Distributed by
Flowerfield Enterprises. Phone: (269) 327-0108
Fax: (269) 327-7009.

Websites

The City Farmer site (www.cityfarmer.org) links to
many other worm sites. We also maintain a complete
list of North American worm suppliers:
<www.cityfarmer.org/wormsup179.html>

CHAPTER 2

Good Bugs, Bad Bugs, and Love Bugs

September 23

Sa-squash Sighting?

Sowbugs are eating our squash. Few believe us. "Sowbugs only dine on seedlings and young bean plants," they say. But we know the truth: those prehistoric pests have sucked up entire lobelia plants. All we need is proof. So we've started sneaking up on the little armadillos, taking photos of the teensy tanks in action. So far, our snapshots are fuzzy and about as convincing as the Sasquatch footage.

Lust and Love at the Garden Gate

You just never know what might happen when you invite art into the garden. After all, art is the perfect mate for the garden. It belongs amid the fruit and flowers: the divinely inspired coupled with the Divine Mother N. Like Cupid and Psyche, they unite heart and soul. It is a relationship that has much to teach us about the art of true loving. In the presence of such a union, one could easily be wooed by bouquets of blood red passion. But heed our counsel: bar this suitor's entrance at the garden gate. Granted the fragrance is intoxicating, but climb into a bed of roses and you'll be stuck with prickly thorns.

LOVE IN THE MIST (*Nigella damascena*)

We needed a new garden gate. It would be both practical and artistic, we decided — working art. I had this vision in my head of a gate sculpted out of old garden tools. I wanted it to lift straight up, high above the garden. By day it would serve as a sign luring people in. By night it would pull down and lock, discouraging night-time prowlers. The search for a metal sculptor began and it wasn't long before Randy from Lovesick Metalworks came a callin'. (The preceding names have been changed to protect the lovelorn.)

It was love at first sight. And not just for me — Wes, our head gardener, was as taken with him as I was. Randy was young, passionate by nature. He's one of us, Wes and I said in a glance. After years of working side by side, we are confident in our combined ability to read people. We know a real city farmer when we meet one. The gate idea excited Randy. With passions aroused and our heads in the clouds, Wes and I plum forgot that love was blind.

Randy lingered with us over the design. "The gate needs a creative solution," we intimated, "to overcome space limitations." It couldn't swing open from the middle like our previous gate because we'd put in an alpine garden on the left. There wasn't enough room for an accordion gate to fold open to the right, either. And because this was our main entrance, we wanted to attract attention. "Come hither," the gate should say. "Learn everything you ever wanted to know about composting and growing food in the city."

When Randy left that day, we were smitten. Head over heels high on him. He's one of us, Wes and I gushed. A real city farmer. He understands us. He sees our vision. He told us he was off to

Hawaii for a couple of weeks and he would call us with the estimate as soon as he got back, then we'd get started. We would count the days.

LOVE LIES BLEEDING (*Amaranthus caudatus*)

We never heard from him again. I left several messages asking him to call us back. Was it the engineering that had scared him off? In hindsight, Randy had seemed a bit nervous about committing to such a grand-scale project. On the final call I pleaded with him to tell us what went wrong. If he didn't want the job, fine, but couldn't we still be friends? Please let us know, I said, so we can move on with our lives. Not a word. I began to have worried fantasies. Had he been hit by an outrigger in Hawaii? Did a coconut fall and knock him unconscious one romantic evening on the beach? Later I heard through the grapevine that he was alive and well and showing at a large garden show in the city. We felt used and abused; it had been a one-afternoon stand.

For a month, Wes and I moped around the garden like jilted lovers, heartsore and pride-bruised. How could we have been so wrong? We're usually such good judges of character. We were mad at ourselves for succumbing to mere chemistry. We've had enough life experience to distrust ephemeral emotions; excitement is destined to wane, eclipsed by a waxing depression. The attraction had been superficial, we admonished one another; it would never have satisfied us. We wanted something deeper, a relationship that would last. Face it, Randy was not meant to be our gate mate.

Finally, Mike, our gentle boss, asked if he could line us up with another metal sculptor he'd found. We kicked at the ground with our garden clogs; well, okay then.

"His name is Davide Pan," Mike said. "Pan, you know," he cajoled, "like the mythic god, symbol of the universe, personification of nature."

Yeah, yeah, we sniffed, and renowned for his escapades with wood nymphs. Nevertheless, we tucked our wounded hearts into our gardening best, and braced ourselves for another liaison. Would the gods smile on us this time?

PEARLY EVERLASTING (*Anaphalis margaritacea*)

When Davide walked through the door, Wes and I retreated into our shells. He didn't look like our type — that is, he was nothing like Randy. Where Randy had been bold, brash, and exciting, Davide was quiet — studied, even. I know he sensed our reticence. Well, we were not about to have our hearts broken again. We proceeded cautiously to the gate site and began to discuss the design with him. Slowly, we began to see beneath his serene surface. This humble, unassuming man would not shy away from an engineering challenge; his resources ran deep.

Warming up, I began to tell him about an exhibit I'd seen recently at a local art gallery. "I think it was called *Show of Hands*," I said. "All these gardening tools hanging on a wall, like a row of arms with large, pendulous plaster hands."

He listened to me quietly, patiently, as I blathered on. Then he said, "That's my work." By the time he left, we knew we had our man. This Pan, this god of flocks and shepherds, woods, and fields, was infinitely more qualified for the job than Randy. Yes, we were in very good hands. He would have the design drawn up and a budget to us in a couple days. Thank heaven, we had met our match.

Davide did come back with the design and the budget, and the gate was completed within a month. Half the neighborhood turned out to watch the installation. He based the gate on our original design, but he brought it to life, sculpting our essence into it. He constructed an old-fashioned metal headboard, measuring ten feet by ten feet (three meters by three meters), to frame the composition. Then he welded together a collage of old gardening tools: pitch forks with curlicue tines, rakes with bolts on their teeth, and wooden-handled shovels. The gate lifts into the sky on a pulley system counterweighted with boulders strapped in metal. These "rocks in bondage" dangle from rusty chains that creak and groan with medieval flair whenever the gate is opened or closed.

People notice us now. Passersby, newspaper and magazine editors, television producers — all are drawn in by the gate. Strangely, the gate looks as if it's always been there. That's how much it belongs, that's how well Davide captured us. Even if our name weren't spelled out in rusty letters atop the gate, it would still say *City Farmer*. People love the gate so much they have invited Davide to make art in their gardens, too. And we've engaged him to help us with other projects.

One day while Wes and I stood musing over the gate, I said, "Well, now we know why Randy didn't work out. He was a bout of fleeting passion, but Davide is slow burning romance."

"Yup," Wes said, "it's the difference between lust and love."

And wouldn't Pan be pleased as punch that we'd learned our lesson. We imagine him peering down at us from his heavenly abode, pine leaves adorning his head, sweet music flowing from the syrinx at his lips. Then with a wink and a nod, he confirms that his own legendary appetites are well in check now, too.

So if you'll permit, a little advice from two who have felt passion's sting: if you invite art into the garden, be prepared for a lesson on love. It seems only right that we learn love's lessons here: relationship is so evident in a garden. Above the hum of ecosystems, life webs, and companion plantings, the gods whisper: true love — whether romantic or platonic, brotherly, sisterly, for friend or humanity — transcends the physical. It seeks a higher image of the human being. It is not a feeling; it is an infinite, unifying force that speaks of the unity of life and the interconnectedness of all things. So go ahead, invite art into the garden, but go thoughtfully, prayerfully even, and stay firmly rooted in the divine, for you are treading on passionate ground.

June 15

The Art of Change

Spence, our garden handyman, built us beautiful new worm bins this spring and now my artist friend, Laurel Sweet, is painting a mural on them for us. Hilary painted the mural on the old ones back in 1995. They were very cute, all sunflowers *and earthy things. We were comfortable with the old granola look.*

After consulting with the worms one afternoon, Laurel did a sketch of her plan; her composition was bright blue with giant yellow worms. It was bold and abstract. Mike and I had simultaneous anxiety attacks; we weren't ready for this leap into our future. We wrung our hands and polled all the staff; we called in neighboring architects and other artist friends. Laurel bore with us patiently. The consensus was that it was time for a change.

Laurel catapulted us into a whole new level of sophistication at the garden. The worm bin mural was a hit with the public, too. So just to show Laurel how sophisticated we were, Mike and I decided to let her paint the storage cupboards, too. We saw her design today: a tiger lily in screaming blues and oranges.

"Color, warmth, and new life, exactly what we need around here," I said artfully. "Right, Mike?"

He nodded enthusiastically, but he was a little pale.

June's Bugs

Ursula can spot a spittlebug from fifty paces. Of course, they're not that hard to spot: just look for gigantic gobs of spit. I'm on my hands and knees listening to a very beneficial guest: Ursula Dole of Greenbug Biological Pest Control. Holy Sowbug, Spiderman, does this woman know her pupae! She was giving a couple of us City Farmers a preview of her upcoming workshop that will be held at our garden this month. I've never had a crawling tour of a garden before and I must admit, there are a lot of shady characters in this verdant underworld.

Spittlebugs are living in our lavender. It's actually the tiny green juvenile bugs hiding inside the spit which produce the spittle.

"It serves as a protection shield," said Ursula in her slight German accent. "This protective 'fart bubble' is secreted from the Anal Clan of the Nymphs."

"Hmmmm, same clan we're from," I whispered to my Ya Ya sister-worker, Jan.

"Take your head set off," Jan shouted. "She said anal *gland* of the nymph."

"The nymph," Ursula interjected loudly, "is the teenage stage of any true bug."

"Are there any predators for those critters?" I asked.

"Only us humans, packing a powerful hose," said Ursula. But as there was no visible damage to our two large, well-established plants, we let the spittlebugs be and crawled on.

We found aphids on the gooseberries. Actually, thanks to the cold wet spring we've had, we found aphids throughout the garden in their many-splendored colors, on the chard and the fava beans. And of course, right alongside these sticky fellas, their industrious companions, the ants.

"Ants and aphids have a symbiotic relationship," explained Ursula. "Aphids secrete honeydew: their poo literally doesn't stink."

Ants love this sweet treat so much that they actually farm the aphids, carrying them away to over-winter in their nests! In our garden, the wise-guy ants were using the nearby chives as a ladder to climb up to the gooseberry. Then they piggybacked the aphids to more convenient snacking locations.

"So how do we take out the aphids?" asked "Bugsy" Jan Malone.

"With a pizza, delivered right to their door," said Ursula. She mixed up some of her all-purpose "pizza spray" and blasted away at the aphids, taking care to spray underneath the leaves. The spray will control the aphids to a certain level, then the beneficials (bugs we want in the garden) will take care of the rest. We decided to track down the rest of the aphid-loving mob.

Ladybugs lap up aphids by the gallon. We spotted some on the sweet cicely and when the sun peeked out, a few more on the black currant bush!

Ursula pointed out the pretty green lacewings on the angelica. "Their larvae are aphid gobblers, too," she said.

As are the larvae of syrphid or hover flies (that annoying fly that circles round and round). Their single oval white eggs are usually laid among aphid colonies. We found some on the cabbages and the cardoon.

Okay, so we had the aphids covered, but the turf wars weren't over yet. There were thrips on the potatoes, good guys and bad guys. Fortunately, the good thrips (dark gray and white striped) eat the bad thrips (yellowish white). These leaf-destroyers can burrow right inside pretty little flower heads. A shot of Ursula's secret all-purpose spray and we crawled on.

We discovered blackspot on the roses. Blackspot is a soil-borne disease and Ursula had a tasty solution that would rejuvenate the plant.

"Mash a rotten banana (with the peel) and mix it with coffee grounds, then bury it at the base of the rose."

She had other fruity cocktails for managing snails and those thugs, the slugs. She even had a mealy concoction for sowbugs, those little prehistoric tanks that drive every gardener buggy.

"Aren't chives a good companion plant for roses?" asked Jan.

"Ya, ya," said Ursula.

Apparently, chives release sulfur that kills fungal diseases and deters pests by masking the scent of the rose. This was just one example of companion planting, an organic gardening strategy that helps to strengthen plants from the ground up.

Just then a beautiful white butterfly twinkled by.

"It's a moth," said Jan.

"It's a butterfly," screamed I.

We turned to Ursula. This argument would be settled once and for all.

"It's a white cabbage butterfly," said my favorite bug inspector. "They help to pollinate the cabbages."

True moths are night owls and don't usually flutter about by day. But the butterfly moth larvae do eat cabbage leaves, so Ursula suggested picking them off at the caterpillar stage and feeding them to the ground beetles lurking in the creeping thyme.

Speaking of creeping, low-growing herbs and shrubs (like our creeping sedum) create a permanent habitat for lowlife, territorial critters such as ground beetles, rove beetles, and spiders. Beetles eat soft-bodied insects like caterpillars, aphids, thrips, slug eggs, cut worms, army worms, and cabbage worms. The small flowers on herbs will attract other beneficials and pollinators, such as parasitic wasps. And the blackberries along our garden fence house numerous beneficials including many birds that peck up aphids, mosquitoes and flies.

Ursula uses a beautiful blend of biological control and organic growing methods to create healthier, happier gardens. Her solutions can be as simple as weeding and thinning, or more complex and creative as with her traps, teas and "safe soaps".

"But first and foremost," she stresses, "if you want healthy plants you start with healthy soil."

During the workshop, we began to see the many symbiotic relationships and the delicate balance in the garden ecosystem. Near the end of our tour, I spotted some white stuff on the lavender leaves. Probably a rare fungus. I tugged Ursula's sleeve and pointed proudly.

She shook her head. "Bird poo."

"Don't give up your day racket," said Jan.

November 4

Drunken Slugs

Sophie from the Parks Board came by today. She's an Integrated Pest Management (IPM) expert. She told us about an entomologist friend of hers who had conducted a little slug-management experiment. She bought several *brands of beer, from high end to swill. Then she set them out in little dishes around her garden to see if slugs would prefer one brand over another. Her conclusion: slugs are not discriminating beer drinkers, so buy them the cheap stuff and save the imports for yourself.*

Hot Tips

Are Sowbugs Taking Over the World?

It would appear they are. We get a lot of calls on this prehistoric pest. Call it sowbug, pillbug, potato bug, wood bug, wood lice, tiny armadillo, indestructible tank, they are a pest! *Common-sense Pest Control* by William Olkowski, Sheila Daar, and Helga Olkowski [Taunton Press, 1991] states that sowbugs and pillbugs are "small decomposers that closely resemble each other. However, sowbugs have two small tail-like appendages that pillbugs lack." Pillbugs are the only ones that curl up in a ball when you poke them.

In general, these critters are beneficial decomposers in the compost bin. However, because they eat decaying organic matter, they can become a problem whenever garden vegetables remain damp and cell walls start to break down. Previously known to suck back strawberries, as well as bean and pea seedlings, these isopods are now munching on just about everything, including flowers. Why? Probably because their population has exploded so much in the past few years: they've had to go outside their usual food source. Their only natural predators are snakes and chickens, which doesn't help us city dwellers much. But here are a few suggestions for controlling the population in your garden.

DRY.

Create drier conditions in problem areas. Also, dry out and sift your compost before you put it on the garden. (Pick out the sowbugs — there's one for the anal retentives.)

WATER.

Watering early in the day gives plants time to dry out before evening.

DIATOMACEOUS EARTH.

A two-inch (five-cm) wide strip of diatomaceous earth sprinkled directly over the row where the seeds have been placed will dry the area enough to discourage sowbugs. (Ha! Not for long in the Pacific Northwest.)

WES' BUCKET METHOD.

Wes used to pick up a bunch of sowbugs from under a piece of wood or other debris and throw them into a bucket of water without a moment of remorse.

CORNMEAL.

Mounds of cornmeal (again, kept dry!) in strategic locations draw the sowbugs (careful, grain also attracts rodents) and appear to destroy some of them (it swells inside their bodies). Torturous, but at least the method concentrates them and then you can always set any survivors free in the woods!

SALSA!

Another suggestion from a caller was to spread salsa in between rows of plants or under wood flats, boards, etc. Mix oil in with the salsa so it doesn't dry out. Don't forget the chips. Olé!

TABASCO SAUCE.

If the salsa isn't hot enough for you, try this one. Use two teaspoons (10 ml) of Tabasco in a quart (one liter) of water as a spray on problem plants/areas.

COMPANION PLANTING.

Some suggested deterrents are: flax, horseradish (plant at corners of beds), or spread dead nettle around the corners of the bed.

SACRIFICIAL CROP.

Plant a crop of tender lettuce around a garden bed — a crop that you intend to sacrifice. The sowbugs will be drawn to the lettuce and will leave what's inside the bed alone. Also, if you leave debris — such as old garden trimmings, a leaf pile, or a rotting stump — in your garden, sowbugs will be drawn to that area and (we hope) will leave your real crops alone!

GENETIC MODIFICATION.

Now if none of these works, there may be a new option coming down the pike. Doug Kilburn, professor emeritus in the microbiology department at the University of B.C., has just retired and has plenty of time on his hands. We are trying to convince him to develop a genetically modified raptor sowbug that will eat its mate. Now there's a match made in heaven.

August 3

Laurachnaphobic

Laura is afraid of spiders. There are certain jobs she refuses to do: cleaning up in the dungeon underneath the greenhouse, cleaning out behind the compost toilet — well, basically cleaning anywhere that is cobwebby, which pretty much rules out any cleaning jobs. It makes for an interesting tour when Laura opens the worm bins for visitors and then screams because she sees a big hairy arachnid.

The Love Garden

It all started with a dream. Mike's dream. One morning Mike woke up (at home, not at the garden) and said to his wife, Joan, "I had a dream. I think Spring might like Barry."

And I did. Although not at first.

Barry was an old friend of Mike's. He had known both of us for almost a decade when he set us up. But matchmaking was not his field and getting messages in a dream was flaky new ground. His inexperience showed.

"I think you might like my receptionist," Mike told Barry on the phone. Never mind that my business card reads: Garden Commander and Goddess of the Hotline. Sensing Barry might need a little more to go on, he added, "She was in advertising and she's polite."

"Sounds promising, but will she pass the shoe test?" Barry wondered.

Fortunately, Joan was an experienced matchmaker; she gave me the goods on Barry. "Tai chi guy, meditator, vegetarian, from New York originally, smart, funny."

"Yeah, but can he compost?" I asked.

Three years without a date and advancing age had seriously shrunk my list. You know what I mean — everyone has a list. Things they will and will not tolerate in a prospective mate. I had two absolute "do not do's." First, I do not do beards. Bald was okay, but no facial hair. Second and even more importantly, I do not do small, stubby hands. My man must without question have beautiful hands, large, with long piano fingers. Budding bellies were fine, but I would not tolerate pudginess in hands.

Our first date was at the garden — take-out Chinese at the picnic table. I had my head in a compost bin when he walked through the garden gate.

"Hello," he said.

I looked up and there he was. Rumpled but stylish New York, with a generous dash of west coast outdoorsman (translation: fleece), and, I recoiled, a beard and mustache. Okay, it's only a date. I glanced down at his hands and blanched. Small, child-like hands — smaller than mine with short stubby fingers and (the gods were laughing now) a missing thumb! Of course, nobody is perfect until you fall in love with them.

"So, do you have a compost bin?" I cut to the chase.

"No, I live in an apartment," he said, "but I thought you might help me set up a worm bin?"

Okay, so I can't write him off completely. By the end of the lunch I was thinking, Hmmm, he's good company. Definitely not my type, but good company. I opened my fortune cookie, it said (and I kid you not): YOU HAVE FOUND GOOD COMPANY, ENJOY! I tucked it into my pocket, just in case.

"Cute boots," Barry said as we parted.

So the garden worked its magic and love blossomed. Now I can't imagine my dream guy without his beard and hands — well, you know what I mean. If this is a dream, I hope Mike never wakes up.

Meanwhile, Mike was strutting around the garden like a seasoned yenta. But maybe our union was a fluke — beginnner's luck? He was anxious to try out his yentic abilities once again. He began pouring through the garden photo albums, in search of potential pairings.

One spring day, Rick walked into the garden. He was a tall, fresh-faced, unsuspecting fellow and he wanted to volunteer. Within minutes of meeting him, Mike was pitching his dating service.

"Once you start volunteering here, we introduce you to our network, see…" He pulled out an album and began showing him prospects. Rick giggled nervously.

"You'll have to excuse him," I explained. "He's had one successful match and he now considers himself a full-fledged yenta."

"One hundred percent success," boasted Mike.

I sent a bewildered Rick out to the back forty to poke — rather, to aerate a compost bin.

"He'd be perfect for Kate," Mike said breathlessly. "She's ripe for romance."

"You're treating our staff and volunteers like your personal stable," I said.

"They're both tall," Mike persisted.

"That's your criteria?" I responded incredulously. "Oh, that's deep."

"It's a match made in heaven," Mike said. "I think I'll just see if Kate can help out this afternoon." He reached for the phone.

There is something about mixing and sifting compost that does stir the heart. I mean all that organic matter teeming with life and fertility. Of course, love can be helped along a little. Whenever Kate and Rick were working together, Mike began locking the two of them into an enclosed section of the garden.

But when I asked Kate how things were going with her and Rick, she said, "Oh, he's nice, but he's not my type."

"Well," I said, "nobody is perfect, until you fall in love with them." Then I told her my tale of the beard and the missing thumb.

A couple weeks later, we heard through the garden grapevine that they'd been on a date. And then another. And another. The garden yenta scores again.

With two successes under his belt, Mike's having brochures done up. "If I get a digital camera, we can put it on our website next," he said.

"Why not set up a video camera and call it Love Garden Cam?" I sniped.

"Not bad," Mike said with a glint in his eye.

He's currently working on romance number three: a neighbor of his who likes glasses and a friend of mine who wears a lot of different glasses.

Okay, so it makes sense that love should happen in a springtime garden with all those bees buzzing, pheromones flying, and tulips opening. But will Mike's matchmaking skills stand up to a dry summer, a dull fall, or a bleak and rainy winter? That will be the true test of the garden yenta and his Dating Service for the Ecologically Minded. Any volunteers?

Hot Calls

SPRING INTO ACTION

Q: Are the thousands of little white bugs inside my worm bin fermentation mites?

A: No, they are springtails. Here's the difference. Springtails are insects with six legs. They feed on organic material and thrive in moist environments. Usually, there's a combination of juveniles (which don't "spring" or jump around) and adults (which do spring). On the other hand, mites (probably mold mites — our bug expert, Ursula Dole, was unfamiliar with the term fermentation mites) are related to spiders and have eight legs and a round body. These mites are so small you would have trouble seeing them, but there are thousands of them in the bins, too. Mold mites eat plant materials like mold, algae, decaying wood, etc. Mary Appelhof has good descriptions of both these critters, complete with illustration, in the revised edition of her book, *Worms Eat My Garbage*. [Flower Press, 1997, pp. 98-102]

October 16

Living Art

Big panic at the garden today. Denise, one of our worm instructors, burst into the greenhouse while I was talking someone through a composting crisis (flies, flies, I've got a million flies, what should I do?). There was a foaming, brilliant yellow mass oozing across our big worm bins in the worm corner. What could it be? It looked like someone had spray painted across the inside lid. Denise, an artist, wanted to do "living art" with it. We had to tie her up while we called our resident biologist/dentist in training, Hilary. She diagnosed it right on the phone! Plasmodial slime mold (PSM).

Wow! PSM is a wood decomposer and needs just the right conditions to thrive. It has been raining for months, so obviously it likes moisture. But Hilary warned us not to just scrape it off (as I wanted to do) because the spores will spread. So we had to wait until it dried and then scraped it off and, I'm sorry to say, threw it into the garbage. Apparently the spores will still spread, but all over the landfill instead of our worm bins. This critter has even been known to climb trees and cross roads! Holy Plasmodial Slime Mold, Batman, sounds like an X-Files episode to me.

Contacts & Resources

ARTISTS

These are some of the artists who have brought their art into our garden.

Clara and Karen Carotenuto
Caro Giardino Design
Phone: (604)328-5893
E-mail: caro.giardino@3web.net
Clara and Karen create beautiful water-catchers, leaves, and stepping stones from concrete imprinted with organic materials such as leaves or twigs. They gifted our garden with a beautiful leaf-shaped bird bath.

David S. Fushtey
E-mail: dfushtey@studio.dsfw.com
Website: <www.studio.dsfw.com>
Dave is a gifted stone sculptor. He believes the best community art is not unlike a garden with layers of meaning and purpose. He designed and built our beautiful dry stack wall under the cherry tree.

Davide Pan
Phone: (604) 255-9796
E-mail: davidepan@hotmail.com
Davide is known internationally for his work with recycled materials. His sculptures, mostly large installations, are part of private and public collections throughout North America and Europe. Davide created two gates for our garden.

Katherine Surridge
Tideline Productions
Phone: (604) 261-2237/(604) 612-8240
E-mail: tideline@telus.net
Website: <www.tidelineproductions.com>

Painter and filmmaker Katherine Surridge uses images from the garden as a metaphor for humankind in relation to the world. Katherine did a series of watercolors on our garden.

Laurel Sweet
E-mail: laurelsweetis@shaw.ca
Laurel's evocative art captures the essence of things. In addition to producing two-dimensional work in acrylic, oil, and gouache, she is also a stone sculptor. Laurel painted the beautiful murals on our worm bins and outdoor storage cupboards.

Pickle Ridge Rustic Carpentry
J-4705 Trans Canada Hwy.
Duncan, BC V9L 6E1
Phone: (250) 748-0763 Fax: (250) 748-2988
E-mail: johnl@pacificcoast.net
Website: <www.pickleridge.com>
This company makes beautiful rustic garden furniture, trellises, archways, and much more. Their furniture is so artistic that I wanted to include them here. We have one of their big swings in our garden.

Books

Cultivating Sacred Space: Gardening for the Soul, by Elizabeth Murray. Pomegranate, 1997

Gardens of Illusion, by Sara Maitland and Peter Matthews. Sterling Publishing, 2000

In Harmony with Nature: Lessons from the Arts & Crafts Garden, by Rick Darke. Friedman-Fairfax, 2000

Websites

Garden Art Gallery. <garden-art.com>
This site features a juried outdoor art exhibition developed by international artists.

Garden Artisans. <gardenartisans.com>
This site features garden art, arbors, trellises, planters, and birdhouses.

Isamu Noguchi Garden Museum. <www.noguchi.org>
For sheer inspiration. This master stone sculptor worked in stone, wood, water, and light.

Suite 101. <www.suite101.com>
This educational site has some wonderful articles and books on art in the garden.

BIOLOGICAL PEST CONTROL

Groups/Organizations

We maintain a list of local organic gardeners and landscapers on the City Farmer website, but check with your landscape and nursery organization to source them in your area. <www.city-farmer.org/orglandscape.html>

B.C. Landscape and Nursery Association
#101 - 5830 176A Street
Surrey, BC V3S 4E3
Phone: (604)-574-7772 Fax: (604)-574-7773
E-mail: bclnainfo@telus.net
Website: <www.canadanursery.com/bclna>

Northwest Coalition for Alternatives to Pesticides
PO Box 1393
Eugene OR 97440-1393
Phone: (541) 344-5044 Fax: (541) 344-6923
E-mail: info@pesticide.org
Website: <www.pesticide.org>

Organic Landscape Alliance
30 Duncan Street, Suite 201
Toronto, ON M5V 2C3
Phone: (416) 596-7989 Fax: (416) 596-0345

E-mail: info@organiclandscape.org
Website: <www.organiclandscape.org>

Books/Publications/Magazines

The Greenbug Guide to a Totally Organic Garden, by Ursula Dole & Dianne VanKirk. B.C. edition. Self-published by Greenbug, Biological Pest Control and Garden Restoration, 1998. To order, call: (604) 733-4638.

Common-sense Pest Control, by William Olkowski, Sheila Daar, and Helga Olkowski. The Taunton Press, 1991

The Bug Book: Harmless Insect Controls, by Helen and John Philbrick. Garden Way Publishing, 1974

Websites

<www.greendecade.org>
A list of American organic landscapers based on the membership of the Ecological Landscapers Association and other organizations can be found here.

<www.wlapwww.gov.bc.ca/epd/epdpa/ipmp/index.html>
The B.C. Ministry of Environment's site for information on Integrated Pest Management (IPM) and landscape pests.

<www.wwf.ca>
The World Wildlife Fund's site has several pesticide reduction press releases.

CHAPTER 3

Garden Gatherings

September 22

The Great Wall of Kitsilano

Dave Fushtey, our friend and stone sculptor, laid the final stone in our dry stack wall beneath the cherry tree last night. What began as a two-week project turned into a three-month marathon. Initially we had a group of volunteers helping out — Wes and Barb, Sharon, Nicholas, Jennifer, and Erica, even Mike got swarthy one day and helped cut a few stones. Erica hung in the longest, but the work party dwindled as the summer wore on. On the final night, Dave was alone — well, Barry and I kept him fueled with pizza and chocolate. The wall is beautiful, though, and it's done just in time for the Compost Tea Party this weekend! Guests will now be able to sit on a rock and a hard place.

The City Farmer Compost Tea Party

Last fall, we threw a giant tea party — the City Farmer Compost Tea Party. The garden was transformed into a bustling marketplace with colorful flags and a bamboo gateway. About 300 people attended the fundraiser, including the gardeners from our Best Food Garden in Vancouver Contest. Guests learned about teas for their plants, their health and the ones you drink for the caffeine hit.

At the Iranian station, Ziba poured from two giant samovars. Guests sat on a bed draped with a Persian carpet, sipping jasmine tea from ornate glasses and eating baklava. Mahen was at the Indian tea stall serving up sweet, milky chai. Barry, our Jewish Chinese tea expert, was brewing woodsy oolong leaves in tiny pots. In another corner of the lush garden, the rustle of silk kimonos meant the Japanese tea ceremony was underway. There was also British tea, green tea ice cream, a Polish tea leaf reader, and a Peruvian musician. It was a world in one garden — Trudeau's vision of Canada. And all it was meant to be was a tea party.

Ever since I hooked up with Barry, my New York Jewish émigré, I've been party to a new Canadian conversation. Like when he took me to my first Seder this Passover. There I was, a small "c" catholic at table with a boy, a lesbian, a black woman, and a handful of Jews eating lasagna with chopsticks.

"Only in Canada," Barry whispered to me.

In this new conversation, boundaries crumble like matzoh, as we harvest the bounty of fresh foods, cultures, and religions.

Melanie, our hostess, held her hands over the candles and sang the opening prayer. We read from a modern version of the Haggadah, which tells the story of the flight of the Jews from Egypt. As we read, and ate the specially prepared foods, we were encouraged to share our thoughts and feelings about all human suffering and liberation, and about the nature of freedom and justice. But all I could think of was, why chopsticks?

At the risk of sounding completely vacuous, I asked, "Why are we eating lasagna with chopsticks?"

"It's a hangover from our hippie days," Bob piped up, "when brown rice was the cure for everything. I think we thought chopsticks were more organic."

Okay, but why lasagna?

Easter Sunday brunch found us in another non-traditional setting — at least, it was a long way from the Russian-German tradition I'd grown up with. The only common thread was that all our extended-family events were centered around food, too. Once again, there was a potluck of cultural backgrounds around the table with the food to prove it: pancakes, bagels and cream cheese, a dim sum selection, frittata, and of course, Belgian chocolate bunnies. As I bit the head off my bunny, the conversation turned multicultural.

"One day a friend and I were meditating in the Chinese Buddhist church where we practice tai chi," Lena said. "Suddenly we were distracted by some native drums and chanting that was going on outside. 'Look where we are!' I whispered to Sarah. 'We're Jewish, for God's sake!' 'Only in Canada,' Sarah said."

"For me it was the richness of being in all those places at once," said Lena. "Come to think of it," she laughed, "most of my best friends are Jewish Buddhists."

A couple of weeks later we were at the Bo Kong, a Buddhist vegetarian restaurant, for Barry's birthday celebration. I looked around the table at our colorful mix of friends: a Japanese couple; a Chinese man and his Caucasian partner; a Scot, and a Norwegian. As the Asian waiters sang happy birthday in heavily accented English, Barry blew out the candles on the mango pudding.

"So, how did you and Terry meet?" I asked Donna, a beautiful Japanese potter.

"We went to school together, but I wasn't attracted to him until he wooed me with dolmathes."

"Dolmathes?" I turned to Terry.

"Just something I picked up on the kibbutz," he said.

"Kibbutz?"

"I went to Hebrew University in Jerusalem," he revealed.

"Why in the world would you go there?" I asked. "Did you want to convert or was it just for the grape leaves?"

"No," he said, "a couple of my buddies were going so I applied for a scholarship and got it."

In fact, he was so naive about Middle Eastern politics at the time that when he was assigned the only Arab student as a roommate, he didn't even realize why. But it was his Israeli experience that led Terry to explore his own roots.

"I wanted to learn more about what it meant to be a Japanese person in Canada. So I moved to Chinatown," he said.

"Chinatown?"

"Right, not many Japanese people there," he said, "but it was a real eye opener for me. I had moved into an Asian culture that was actually flourishing. There were hundreds of Chinese people just buying their bok choy and gai lan. Oy vay! Maybe it's time I went to Japan."

Meanwhile, back at the Tea Party, Sharon Slack, our new head gardener, and I awarded prizes to the winners in our Best Food Garden contest. Mr. Calogero's garden took up two back yards and most of a front yard; it was plum full of tomatoes, chicory, peppers, and basil. In Mr. Arruda's garden there were grafted pear and apple trees and an orangery in his greenhouse. Magdalena Marcos grew a "Three Sisters" garden: black corn, beans, and squash. As the gardeners walked off with their trellises and butterfly feeders, I glanced at the gai lan and bok choy flourishing in our own little patch of land. Diversity is healthy in a garden.

So on the surface at least, it seems that Canada is a pretty tolerant place where you can do and be a whole bunch of things without anyone making too much of a fuss. In Vancouver at any rate, we can cross eat, cross dress, or cross-pollinate. We are not bound by race. We can openly explore other cultures. We're all observers and participants. So a Jewish guy can be a Chinese tea expert. A Scotsman can serve tea in a kimono instead of a kilt. A Polish tea leaf reader can study tai chi with a Chinese master. And a compost hotline operator can eat lasagna with chopsticks. Vive le jardin!

Hot Teas

CITY FARMER COMPOST TEA

We fill a burlap sack about a quarter full with premium black gold or fin-ished compost and set it into a five-gallon (18.75-liter) pail and fill with water. Brew for about a week and use.

BARNYARD TEA COMPANY

Here's a great product that inspired City Farmer's Compost Tea Party: Barnyard Tea. This "composted manure tea" is packaged in standard tea bags so you can brew up a batch for your plants without muss or fuss. This Canadian company has devised a way to dry organic manure, pre-serving nutrients and removing all odors. It has all the macro- and micro-nutrients in it, as well as a number of beneficial bacteria and other organisms that plants love. Look for it in high-end gardening stores or catalogues like Lee Valley Tools (<www.leevalley.com>), Garden Talk (<www.gardentalk.com>), and Johnny's Seeds (<www.johnnyseeds.com>). Visit their website at <www.barnyardtea.com>

June 15

Crazy About Garden Tours

Three of us garden gals took a field trip to funky Denman Island for their famous annual garden tour. North of Victoria, the island is home to many artists, writers, and nature lovers. The highlight for us was our visit to the fable-like cottage home of Des Kennedy, author of Living Things We Love to Hate and Crazy About Gardening. One of our favorite features was the two-seater compost toilet where you can actually sit knee to knee with your beloved. Jan explained to me that the paired toilets were not so much communal as practical: when one hole fills up, they can switch over to the other. And here I thought it was the love toilet.

The Many Senses Garden Tour

I went on a garden tour on a glorious spring afternoon, fully expecting an assault on my senses. I wasn't disappointed. The air was laden with the deep purple scent of wisteria; the sky paint-splashed with vibrant yellow laburnum; bird songs filled my ears. But even my sixth sense did not prepare me for the unfamiliar sense I would encounter in the garden.

It was Salmonberry Days in Dunbar — a quaint, quiet, well-established neighborhood in Vancouver's southwest corner. The annual month-long celebration of community was organized by the proactive Dunbar Residents' Association. Through May, residents and visitors can take part in nature walks and talks, a fun run, an art show, and a garden tour that stretches over two weekends.

My friend Judith Cowan and I arrived at our first stop, lured in by the tantalizing guide description "shady Pacific Northwest native garden with pond and waterfall." But sadly, a sign posted to the gate informed us: This garden not open today, please check your map. Aha, this garden had only been open on one of the designated tour days. Can you sense our disappointment? We tried to peek over the fence, but alas — the sound of falling water tickled our ears but gave us no sense of the site.

The next stop was a few blocks east and there was much to savor along the way. We sang the praises of the berry-pink hawthorns, but only until the delicate dogwoods danced into view. All of the 12 gardens on the tour that day were clustered together and easily accessible by foot or car. As we toured, we kept brushing up against some of the same people. Gardeners of all levels, neighbors mostly, a few with company in tow. We lingered over four gardens that afternoon, but faster tour mates easily covered eight.

We knew the people at this next place, Sharon and Terry Slack. They had a large pond that used a type of non-porous clay called bentonite to create a natural muddy-bottom liner. I stooped to inspect the bog area around the pond. It featured delicate natives and edibles like cranberries, blueberries, sundews, salal, and deerferns. Dragonflies hovered, on the hunt for errant mosquitoes. I glanced up at the water gushing over the natural rocks just as a resident hummingbird zipped in for a sip. There was an entire ecosystem in their back yard, including the common variety, two-legged gardeners.

Organizers estimate that up to six hundred people tour the Dunbar gardens during this annual event. Sharon and Terry had 80 visitors that day alone — without losing their sense of humor! Up on the roof garden, Sharon showed off her abundant crop of lettuces, garlic, shallots, and potatoes nestled in straw, then loaded up her grateful guests with pots of peppers.

At our next location, we found another pond, teensy in comparison, but ever so sweet. This pond used a traditional plastic liner, its edges softened by low-growing saxifrage, green heuchera, lemon thyme, and a black leaf clover. A crowd of now familiar faces had gathered around the pond's centerpiece, a white tree peony. In the presence of such beauty, conversation bloomed. We stumbled over Latin names, made up common names, and found we had things in common. It wasn't just the hot afternoon sun that warmed our spirits: we were basking in the glow of fellowship.

In the woodsy area at the back of the yard, the hostas were gigantic and (we sensed) happy alongside the hellebores and trillium.

"What's that tree?" Judith pointed excitedly to an exotic looking conifer.

"Let's ask," I said.

We spotted the owner, over by the fence digging up some pulmonaria for a delighted visitor.

"A Japanese Umbrella," he said. "I'll look up the Latin name for you." And he was off.

People were downright neighborly. All day long, proud but humble gardeners generously opened their yards to strangers, sharing growing tips and plant cuttings. It was in this convivial atmosphere that I felt the unfamiliar sense fully awaken in me. It wasn't an easy sense to evoke in this age of isolation. The last time

I'd hung out with neighbors like this was several years ago on a bright cold January day in downtown Stanley Park, when Lost Lagoon froze over (temporarily displacing the ducks), and half the city turned out to skate. It felt good to chat with neighbors especially in a garden on a sunny afternoon.

Ah, I sighed contentedly, I could name it now. It was my sense of community that had been restored.

January 8

Kumquat May

Jan and I are now sharing a box of organic vegetables which we have delivered weekly to her door through a local company. They get the produce mostly from local farmers. It's great fun. They deliver it in the middle of the night (so no one knows we eat organic vegetables, I presume). I always phone ahead to find out what we're getting. But Jan likes to be surprised. So naturally I call her with annoying clues (What's tiny and orange and rhymes with robot?)

In a comparative shopping study, the Can$ 33 box of vegetables would be $25 at Safeway (but would not be organic) and would be $49 at a local health food chain. So we're saving money — and it's making me cook more and try new recipes. Also I get to try fruits and vegetables I might not normally buy, like oyster mushrooms or kumquats. Actually, I like to say kumquat more than I like to eat it.

Midnight in the Garden of City Farmer

This Hallowe'en story begins in a late summer garden. One of our volunteers, Jennifer, had decided to cast a Bosnian bee-charming spell. She studied Bosnian folklore at university and considered herself qualified.

"Usually you would cast this spell in the spring, to call the bees to the fields, gardens and orchards," she explained, "but the beans I planted haven't been pollinated, I'm going to give it a try."

"But it's the end of August," I said, "what if the spell only works in season?"

"Oh, hocus pocus, what's a couple of months," she said.

On the designated day, our staff gathered around Jennifer amidst the nodding dahlias and pungent mums. There was nary a bee in sight when she began.

"The song is called Pcelice and we address the bees as mothers and sisters. There are three parts to the charm. First, I sing."

Jen began to sing some unintelligible words in a lilting, high-pitched voice. Then she stopped abruptly. "Actually, I don't remember the words, but I think it's more in the tone. Okay, now I must whistle while rubbing two small stones together." So she whistled and clicked and the spell was cast.

In the ten years I've been working here, I've never been stung. I work in a greenhouse office that opens out onto the garden. Bees and wasps fly in and out and around my head all day long. Come to think of it, I can't even remember any of our gardeners getting stung.

The day after Jennifer cast the spell, I was working at my desk when a bee plopped on my neck and stung me good. My boss, Mike, got it next, then Sharon, our head gardener, followed by a volunteer and several environmentalists who share the building with us. One September day, as I was chatting with Jeff, one of our city funders, a bee dropped onto his head and stung him as he brushed it off. My God, they're stinging the hands that feed us!

I called Jennifer, mad as a hornet. "Bees are falling like flies. We need the antidote quick. Our funding could be at stake!"

"I don't know the antidote. I'll look into it. But maybe the spell will just wear off," Jen said hopefully.

And it did — well, at least the stinging spree stopped. But then people began to act strangely. I started to garden. Unusual behavior for me, as I never leave my desk. I was digging up beds faster than Boots, our big bad garden cat, was. Sharon was not amused.

But Sharon was acting weird too. Usually an animal lover, she began blasting away at cats, squirrels, raccoons, and stray environmentalists with a bazooka-size water gun.

"I can give a starling a shower at 40 paces with this thing," Sharon said with a gleam in her eye.

Mike, usually tighter than Jack Benny, began to spend money like he was me. "What should we buy today?" he said. "Money is no object. You want a new porch with a swing? A hot tub in the greenhouse. You name it, it's yours."

The volunteers stopped volunteering and the environmentalists began to smoke and strew garbage about. We heard through the grapevine that Jeff, normally a recluse, had taken off on a two-month cruise.

"We can't wait any longer," I announced to Mike and Sharon. "I can't get any work done I'm so busy gardening. Mike, you've blown half of next year's budget already and Sharon is waterlogging the entire wildlife population here. We'll just have to conjure up our own little anti-bee-charming ceremony."

I called everyone, including the only two people who hadn't been stung: Wes, our former head gardener who arose out of retirement, and Jennifer, the self-appointed Garden Goddess. They would lead the ceremony.

"Midnight, in the Garden of City Farmer," I told them. "Come disguised. The neighbors will think we're having a Hallowe'en party. Bring candles. We'll gather round the Earth Machine."

One by one they came. Wes was dressed as a scarecrow and carried a compost aerator and a jug of wine. Jen wore flowing goddess robes and carried a giant bean pod. Sharon had transformed into Shee-Rahn Slick, eco-warrior princess. Mike was dressed as a hotline operator; he looked fetching in fleece and a headset. I was in coveralls, straw in my teeth, a true city farmer now. Even the volunteers were someone else. We all lit our candles from the cigarettes of the smoking environmentalists, then we encircled the compost bin. We looked to Wes and Jen for direction while Boots (did I mention he's a black cat?) lurked in the shadows.

Wes cleared his throat, took a swig of the "altar" wine, and looked up at the stars. "Hmmm, the planetary influences are favorable," he pronounced. "Bountiful Creator, please accept our gifts and help us to set right the bee-charming spell gone awry with this ancient composting ceremony I discovered."

He opened an old book. "To the usual brown and green composting materials we must add ingredients from this ancient recipe," he said.

I took a closer look. "You brought a book of short stories?" I asked.

"Yes, the recipe is modeled on a method of composting created by Robert Graves," said Wes.

"The guy who wrote I Claudius?" I asked with dismay.

"Well, it was actually one of his characters who came up with the recipe, Dr. Steinpilz," Wes said.

"Oh, well then, we're in good hands," I said.

"It's the best I could come up with on short notice," said Wes.

"Let's give it a try," I said.

Wes stuck his nose back into the book. "Dr. Steinpilz's formula produced extremely fierce bacteria, capable of breaking down an encyclopedia or an old boot."

"You hear that, Boots?" Shee-Rahn called out.

"Have you got the "mother mix," Jen, er I mean, Goddess?" Wes asked.

Jennifer stepped forward with a ram's horn full of goop. "Here it is, Supreme Scarecrow," Jen said. "It's supposed to be a mixture of pulverized animals including a bull's foot and a goat's pancreas, but I used tofu dogs."

Wes nodded approvingly.

"Now the herbs: milkwort, pennyroyal, bee orchid, and vetch," Jen continued, "and a black cat."

"Here kitty, kitty," Sharon's shrill voice rang out.

"I think it's enough that there's a cat in the vicinity," Wes said.

"Okay, let's see now," Wes said, peering into his book. "The final secret ingredient — a virgin, we need a virgin."

He looked out into the weathered faces of the city farmers. "Hmmm. Okay, how about a virgin primrose?" asked Wes.

"There's one here in the garden," said Jen. "It's never been plucked." She handed him a single, quivering primrose.

"That'll do," said Wes. "According to Steinpilz, this delicate flower will be relished by the fierce bacteria. Okay, now we'll mix this baby up," Wes said, reaching for his compost aerator and his wine bottle.

As Wes mixed and drank, Jen began to perform a wild dance around the bin, shaking a giant desiccated bean pod over it and at the surprised congregation. "It's a de-fertility dance," she explained.

"If everyone will join me in the final chanting refrain and sway with me now," Wes said. "Ohhhhhmmmmm, make it wet and dry, make it slimy and obscene, make compost and reverse the bee charm-ing, thing, hiccup."

Everybody joined in, not exactly swaying, but shivering in the cold October air. We gazed silently, expectantly, at the compost bin and then—

"Hey, I hope no one thinks they're getting paid to be here," Mike said.

And so everything returned to normal at the City Farmer garden. Well, almost everything. We've spotted the odd smoking environmentalist and Sharon is still occasionally seen chasing Boots through the garden.

[If you want to find out more about Dr. Steinpilz's unorthodox composting methods, read "Earth to Earth" from *The Shout and Other Stories* by Robert Graves (Penguin Books, 1978, pp. 52–56).]

November 24

Where There's Smokers, There's Fires

We're in the middle of the Asia Pacific Economic Conference (APEC) and hundreds of anti-APEC protesters convene in our building. All the leading environmentalists are here. Our front line comrades: eco-warriors who strap themselves to trees just to save a forest, crusaders out saving the lungs of the earth. But...but...I protest, you've never seen so many smokers in your life. We're still picking butts out of the bergamot.

Hot Tips

THE GREAT PUMPKIN PICK-UP

So what do you do with the pumpkin after Hallowe'en? The first option is to chop it up really well and put it into the compost bin with a little soil and some leaves. Apartment dwellers can add their chopped pumpkins to their worm bin. If you don't have a compost bin but you do have a yard, you can try trenching. Dig a hole at least 18 inches (45 cm) deep, drop in the chopped pumpkin, and cover lightly with garden lime. Then immediately fill in the hole with the excavated soil to prevent a rat invasion. If none of those options work, you can always ask a neighbor or a local community garden if they might take your pumpkin.

We don't recommend using Hallowe'en pumpkins for cooking after the event because they mold quickly and there's usually soot and wax in them. But make sure you scoop out the flesh of the pumpkin beforehand and use it in soups and stews. The seeds are wonderful toasted, too.

Residents in several communities have taken a very festive approach to pumpkin recycling. The day after Hallowe'en, people are encouraged to drop off their pumpkins at designated community center parking lots, creating a mountain of orange. Pig farmers then wheel in and pick up the free pumpkins to feed to their pigs. Volunteer work crews haul the rest away to be composted at the nearby landfill. So if there are pig farmers in your area, you might call and ask if they'd like some Hallowe'en hog feed.

In Vancouver, we're fervently hoping that the city will initiate the Great Pumpkin Pick-up. They would have to make an exception (currently food waste is not permitted) and allow residents to place their pumpkins in their yard-waste containers in the week following Hallowe'en.

And for those who love facts, the world's largest pumpkin to date weighed in at 1337 pounds (594 kg) on October 2002 and was grown in Manchester, New Hampshire. You'd need a crane to pick up that pumpkin and more than 100 bins to compost it.

TRICKS OR TREATS IN THE COMPOST BIN

Don't be tricked by all the composting myths that abound, such as never put banana peels, orange rinds, or unsalted sunflower seed hulls (salted ones should be thrown out) into your bin. Rubbish! In our humble opinion, it is safe and desirable to throw any of these treats into your bin. But no Hallowe'en candy, please!

We also get quite a few calls on the hotline regarding materials that are supposedly poisonous and should not be put in the compost bin. Rhubarb leaves are the first that come to mind. Although the leaves may be toxic to other plants, we have no problem putting them into our compost bins. (You'll find arguments for and against in the literature, though.) No plant or animal has keeled over in our garden yet. Just don't eat the leaves.

The only tricky materials we don't put into the bin are blighted plants (like tomatoes) and pernicious weeds (like buttercup and morning glory). Avoid black walnut leaves as they secrete a toxic tannin (juglanic acid) that can hinder the growth of certain plants and inhibit microbial activity. And we probably wouldn't risk putting in poison ivy or poison oak — or anything else that might make us blotchy and itchy. If anyone has heard otherwise, speak your poison now.

Hot Calls

STRAW BALES AND SCARECROWS

Q: What's the difference between straw and hay?

A: We called up W&A Farms in Richmond, B.C., to get their expert opinion. Hay is usually still green (although sometimes dry and brown) with the seed heads still intact. Hay is used as animal bedding and feed and is great for stuffing scarecrows. Straw is just the tubes of grain stalks, dried and yellowish in color with no seed heads. Straw is preferable to use in the bin, as it is a richer carbon source with less sprouting potential once the finished compost is used on the garden. We usually buy oat straw or clover straw at about Can$ 6 a bale. Straw bales make great seats for outdoor Hallowe'en parties too!

Contacts and Resources

GARDEN TOURS

A quick google search will give you a lifetime of garden tours. But the best way to find out about garden tours in your area is to check with your local botanical garden, gardening groups and gardening magazines; watch the local paper; or ask a gardening friend.

Groups/Organizations

Washington State Federation of Garden Clubs
19408 76th Ave SE
Snohomish, WA 98296
Phone: (360) 668-6111
E-mail: janel@garnettco.com
Website: <www.washingtongardenclubs.org>

BC Council of Garden Clubs
680 Florence Street
Coquitlam, BC V3J 4C6

Phone: (604) 931-1113 Phone: (604) 524-1529
E-mail: bernie.booth@3web.net
Website: <www.gardenwise.bc.ca/gardenwise/garden-clubs.lasso>

Books/Publications/Magazines

I have listed just a few of my favorite books here from our own gardening community.

A Grower's Choice, by Michael K. Lascelle. Raincoast Books, 2001

Canadian Gardens, by David Tarrant. Whitecap, 1994

Crazy About Gardening: Reflections on the Sweet Seductions of a Garden, by Des Kennedy. Whitecap Books, 1994

Garden City: Vancouver, The Ultimate Guide to Everything Green in Vancouver and the Lower Mainland, by Marg Meikle and Dannie McArthur. Polestar, 1999

Living Things We Love to Hate: Facts, Fantasies, and Fallacies, by Des Kennedy. Whitecap Books, 1994

100 Best Plants for the Coastal Garden: The Botanical Bones of Great Gardening, by Steve Whysall. Whitecap Books, 1998

The New Twelve Month Gardener: A West Coast Guide, by Elaine Stevens, Jane Mitchell, Ann Buffam, Dagmar Hungerford and Doris Fancourt-Smith. Whitecap Books, 2000

Websites

I Can Garden. <www.icanGarden.com>
In addition to Canadian information on gardening, you'll also find some garden tours, European-style.

Canadian Gardening.
<www.canadiangardening.com/html/clubs.html>
This gardening magazine website maintains a
comprehensive list of garden clubs and groups
across the country.

National Garden Clubs. <www.gardenclub.org>
This U.S. nonprofit group has membership in
50 states. Log on to find a garden club in your
area.

COMPOST TEAS

Companies

Barnyard Tea Company
P.O. Box 1275
Aldergrove, BC V4W 2V1
Phone/Fax: (604) 732-4668
E-mail: info@barnyardtea.com
Website: <www.barnyardtea.com>

Soil Foodweb Inc.
1128 NE 2nd Street, Suite 120
Corvallis, OR 97330
Phone: (541) 752-5066 Fax: (541) 752-5142
Web: <www.soilfoodweb.com>
Dr. Elaine Ingham is the authority on compost
teas. She has a couple of manuals worth ordering:
The Compost Tea Brewing Manual and the
Soil Biology Primer.
She also has CDs and videos.

Websites

Growing solutions. <www.growingsolutions.com>
A compost tea equipment manufacturer.
Phone: (425) 806-9941.

Soil Soup. <www.soilsoup.com>
Another compost tea equipment manufacturer.
Phone: (206) 542-9304.

CHAPTER 4

Yard Waste Yarns

July 17

Sally Scissorhands

Sally is scissor happy. She's our resident master gardener and flower expert. Normally, she's motherly and nurturing, but put a set of pruning sheers in her hand and she's ruthless. Staff fear for their hair in her presence.

"I think it's time we pruned the clematis," she said today in her cheery voice.

"Well, yes, Sally, but remember what happened with the pyracantha," I said. It used to be a big, beautiful, bushy tree, now it looks like a Tinker Toy. "Don't worry," she sing-songed soothingly. "All will be well and all will be well and every manner of tree will be well."

She snapped her sheers in anticipation. Then she began to prune the clematis. Leaves flew, branches spewed, until we were both hidden in a storm of jackmanii flakes. When the dust settled, the clematis looked more like creeping *thyme than a climbing vine.*

"Nice work, Scissorhands," I said. "Edward would be proud of you."

Confessions of a Lawn Moron

I hate grass. At least I did. I'd spent years cultivating my position on grass. For over two decades we've been teaching people how to grow food — on rooftops, balconies, and boulevards, in school yards, front and back yards, and hospitals. So when people called me on the compost hotline, stressed over lawn laced with dandelions and buttercup, I'd tell them, "Rip it up. Plant some thyme. Grow wild strawberries. Pot up potatoes. Grow something useful. That needy, pampered green mat just lies around, sucking back gallons of water between weekly manicures. It guzzles expensive synthetic fertilizers and pesticides, then pees them out all over the environment." So, karmically speaking, it was just a matter of time before I would be teaching others how to grow beautiful, healthy lawn.

Landfills across the country are closing and water supplies are at an all-time low across the continent, the headlines say. In Las Vegas, they'll give you cash if you rip out your grass to conserve water. Lawn watering accounts for up to 40% of domestic water usage in the dry summer months when supplies are lowest.

"We need to get into grass," my boss Mike said with missionary zeal. "Chemical lawn care is wreaking havoc on the environment. There's got to be a better way."

Inspired by the very successful natural lawn care program in Seattle, he dragged me on a field trip across the line. Obviously he was hoping I'd find grass a little greener on the other side. As we pulled up to the border, my palms began to sweat.

I whispered urgently to Mike, "Do not say the word grass, DO NOT."

"What's the purpose of your visit?" the customs officer asked.

"Mulching mowers," Mike said. I giggled.

The customs guy looked at us suspiciously. "You're buying a mulching mower?"

"No, just looking. There's a truckload of them in a parking lot in Seattle," Mike tried to explain.

I giggled again. Mike choked back a laugh. The customs officer leaned into the car.

"The City of Seattle has sold 4,000 mulching mowers a year for the last six years this way," Mike sputtered. "We want to get people to leave their clippings on the lawn in Canada, too."

"Whassa matter, you afraid to say grass?" the customs guy asked.

Safely back in Vancouver, Mike decided to launch a natural lawn care program here.

I resisted. "People will talk," I said. "After all, what's an urban agriculture group doing promoting lawn care?"

"Look, we're just talking to people about the things we've always been talking about," he said, "using natural fertilizers, cutting down on water, and when we've got them hooked, we can still suggest they dig up some turf and plant an edible landscape."

Reluctantly, I dragged my ass into grass. I was as green as they come on the subject. A complete lawn moron, I'd never even pushed a lawn mower before. So when I wheeled out our skookum electric mulching mower to mow the garden boulevard, I was nervous. Mike trotted alongside me, coaching me, keeping me from trees and small children. These mulching mowers fire the clippings down hard into the soil, feeding the lawn naturally and leaving no mess on the surface. When a neighbor walked by pushing a baby carriage, she looked at us curiously.

"It's her first time," Mike explained.

She nodded. "Mine, too."

As I got deeper into the field of grassology, I realized how obsessed people are with their lawns. Americans spend 45 billion a year on maintenance. It's the largest crop in the U.S., larger than wheat or corn. Apparently we Canucks are just as lawn crazy as the Yanks. This summer, under severe water restrictions, Victorians began painting their lawns green to maintain the status quo! Is lawn just about keeping up with the Jones' — or does it have a higher purpose?

I consulted the grass gurus. Aside from having a playground for your kids and pets, grass does serve a purpose. This rather inexpensive ground cover converts carbon dioxide into oxygen; prevents soil erosion and dust storms; retains moisture and keeps things cool; cuts down on noise and glare; and is a lot nicer to look at than cement. And personally, I find the base of their tender white stems quite tasty. Perhaps grass is good — in moderation.

The more I learned about lawn, the more preoccupied I became. Obscure grass lore haunted me. I heard that raccoons roam the streets at night rolling up newly laid sod, looking for grubs. As a family of raccoons had moved in behind the garden and we had just laid a small test patch of sod there, I began to fret. Should I nail the stuff down? Bungy cord it? Use crazy glue? How do you raccoon-proof your lawn? My obsession followed me into my sleep.

The dream opens on the Grass Man (a truly laid-back west coast mascot) and his sidekick, JoJo the Drum Majorette. The Grass Man wears a mask, grassy vest, and chaps. JoJo sports an artificial turf busby and tosses a lawn baton into the air. The dynamic duo cruise the city on a solar-powered ridem mower ferreting out unnatural lawn care practices and blowing the whistle on water sprinkling violators. Law(n)-breakers are served with papers on natural lawn care and alternative ground covers. Prizes are awarded to true lawn naturalists; the grand prize is a trip for two to Grassland aboard a Flying Lawn Mower.

I woke up. Hmmm, could the dream become reality?

And so, with help from the city of Vancouver, our natural lawn care program was realized. You may already have seen the Grass Man around town, on bus shelters, in TV ads, and a short film at the Ridge, a local repertory cinema. He's been spotted in the flesh at Science World and other grassy knolls around Vancouver. Wherever he goes, people cry out, "Who is that grassed man?"

"Why I'm the Grass Man," he replies. "And I'm on a crusade to save water and cut down on the fertilizers and pesticides polluting our environment. Prepare for natural lawn care!"

I can't help but want a companion for the Grass Man, though, and am plotting ways to bring JoJo to life. I'm thinking a half time show at Nat Bailey Stadium, Vancouver's baseball park with a real grass field. Picture it: The Grass Man rides out onto the field on his grassmobile; JoJo marches alongside him, her Q-tip hat bobbing with every beat of her drum. Behind them, in perfect glide step, the Mulching Mower Marching Band, all pushing mowers in flawless formation, chanting:

Mow it more and mow it high.
Leave your clippings where they lie.
Water less or not at all
Sprinkle compost in the fall.

I love grass. But I'll take mine with a side of tomatoes, please.

Hot Tips

SIX GRASSY STEPS

Natural lawn care takes less time than all that raking and bagging. By doing less, you actually do more. You'll have a healthier lawn, reduce your water use, and prevent those nasty chemicals from polluting our environment.

- Mow high and mow often. Never cut more than one third of the blade — removing too much weakens the grass and makes it more susceptible to disease.
- Leave your clippings on the lawn. The grass you leave behind is a natural fertilizer.
- Water only once a week during the growing season — or better yet, not at all. If you let your lawn get a tan in the summer, it will green up again nicely in the fall.
- Aerate (punch many tiny holes in) your lawn to promote better water drainage. There are more high tech machines, but you can get nifty

shoes with spikes to walk around on the lawn from Lee Valley Tools (see below).

- Sprinkle some compost on the lawn (after aerating) in the spring and again in the fall. Liming in the fall is a good idea, too, if your soil tends to be acidic, as it does in the Pacific Northwest.
- Put up with a few "weeds" — dandelions and clover actually help feed your lawn by pulling up nutrients through their deep roots. So let Creeping Charlie and Veronica make splendor in your grass.

May 23

Grass-essorize

Now that lawn is back in fashion at the garden, we've been grass-essorizing (translation: shopping at Lee Valley Tools). We've got quite the collection — dandelion diggers in various sizes, water-powered weeders, fire-breathing ones, manual power rakes, edgers. But of all the grass gadgets, the aerator sandals are my favorite. Strap them on (okay, it did take four of us to figure out how to put them on and keep them on) and dance your lawn back to natural health. Slip into these spiked heels for your next garden party and sparks will fly.

The Christmas Tree Shredding Ceremony

I'm serious about recycling, especially the composting variety. As City Farmer's Compost Hotline Operator, I have to be. Still, I always try to find the lighter side of garbage. But is there a shred of humor in Christmas tree recycling? Apparently the Japanese think so.

Recently, a caller told me about a taped episode of Japanese "reality television" that he'd seen at a karaoke party. This popular game show travels the world filming staged and real events. The contestants must then determine which events are true to life. That's how our city of Vancouver Christmas Tree Recycling program became famous in Japan.

As I heard it, the segment opens at the Vancouver landfill in Delta where we are about to witness a bizarre Christmas ritual. Even in Japan, West Coasters are known to be environmentally sensitive, so naturally we take our tree "burials" very seriously. Performing the sacred rites were: Garbage Head, Paul Henderson; Angel Singh from the Parks Board; and the Reverend Rudolph, who had a very shiny nose. The three, dressed in fur-trimmed hard hats and flowing fleece robes, clustered around the tree chipper which was bedecked with flashing icicle mini-lights.

While Paul picked a few strands of tinsel off the tree, Angel Singh wrestled with the stand that was stuck to its trunk. Finally, they fed the tree lovingly into the mouth of the shredder and hit the switch. In a flurry of chips and artificial snow, the Reverend began to shout solemnly.

"We are gathered around this Christmas tree, so evergreen have its branches been, to honor this king of the woodland scene. Once the pride of the mountain side, then cut down to grace our Christmas tide." He lit some incense and waved it over the half-shredded tree. "And now as we shred you in your winter prime, may you bring new life in verdant spring time."

Rudy wiped his runny, shiny nose. "Please join me in singing, Oh Christmas Tree."

Paul and Angel Singh sang along. Then they each lit a candle and planted it in the little pile of wood chips that was the Christmas tree. The ceremony ended in a moment of silence.

Okay, so if you were a contestant, you'd think the landfill ritual was a hoax, right? That's what I thought, too, until I started digging a little deeper. I called a couple of members of the Lions Club (the charity that runs the city's neighborhood chipping events) to check the rumor out. Both members danced around my question. I talked to Brian Johnston first.

"Have you heard about this bizarre Christmas tree shredding ceremony they've been performing at the Vancouver landfill?" I asked.

"Oh, that rumor has been circulating since we started the program in the early 90s. I can't say if it's true."

"You can't or you won't?" I pressed.

"Well, people do seem to believe in this annual recycling rite. Some of them go to a lot of trouble to get their trees to us at the local chipping events," he said.

According to Brian, some bungy-cord it to their bikes; others harness the trees to their dogs and drag it in husky-style. Last year someone stuffed their tree into a garbage can on wheels and roller-bladed behind it.

"So do you believe there's a blessing ceremony?" I asked.

"Well, if you watch the kids' faces when their trees are being chipped and see them wave good-bye with their little mittened hands…" Brian's voice broke with emotion. "I guess for them it is a little like having their trees blessed before we return them to the earth."

When I asked Terry McKenzie, another Lions' Club member, the same question, she too was evasive.

"Well, we don't do anything too weird at the chipping events," she said. "We put up our own little Christmas tree and hang all the forgotten decorations on it."

"Have you ever had any unusual things left on the trees?" I asked.

"Oh sure, haven't you ever received a gift you'd like to shred? We get the odd mouth-retainer, too, but my personal favorite was the pair of French kissing hens."

Okay, not much help there. I decided to go straight to the source. I called up Paul Henderson at the Vancouver landfill.

When I asked him about the ceremony, he said, "Look, all I'll say is this. People want to know that their trees' lives haven't been sacrificed in vain, that they've served a purpose greater than a light rack. Over the years, we've recycled hundreds of thousands of Christmas trees and their remains are composted in our yard-waste composting facility here at the landfill. That product is then spread around Vancouver parks and sold to landscapers and residents as a rich organic fertilizer. If that isn't a higher purpose, I don't know what is."

"Do you have a copy of the tape?" I asked, anxious for proof that this ceremony existed.

"I did have a tape," he said. "But I lent it to a friend of mine to take to a karaoke party."

"And?" I said.

"The VCR ate it. Yup, not a shred of evidence left."

So you decide: reality or fiction? Personally, I choose to believe in the Christmas Tree Shredding Ceremony. It reminds me of the time that, with hands on hips, I asked my mother, "Is there or is there not a Santa Claus?"

And she replied, "For those who believe, there is."

Hot Tips

CHRISTMAS TREE RECYCLING

Reduce waste and help a local charity by recycling your Christmas tree this year. Many communities have Christmas tree shredding events now. Check your local paper to find one in your area. Usually only live, cut Christmas trees are accepted (no artificial or potted trees). Tinsel and decorations (including French hens) must be removed.

You might also consider decorating a large indoor house plant instead of a cut tree, or buy a potted tree and then perform your very own planting ceremony in the yard after Christmas.

April 16

Wes' Favorite Green Layer

David Tarrant, host of the television program *Canadian Gardener*, arrives with his crew to shoot a segment on our Y2K Victory garden with Wes. When David notices the green shag carpet on top of the compost bin he asks, "So do you always put carpet on your bins?"

"Oh yes," replies the ingenuous Wes, "I always cover my piles."

Uh huh. The amazing Preparation Green Shag retains heat and moisture, while it relieves the pain and itch of composting.

Hot Calls

URBAN BLIGHT

Q: Can blighted plants like tomatoes be put into the municipal green-waste stream for composting or should I throw them out?

A: According to Paul Henderson at the Vancouver landfill, this type of diseased material is fine to bring to the green-waste drop-off (or put out at curb side) as the disease is killed off in the thermophilic process of the large-scale system. So any diseased materials, and even plants or weeds with seed heads, are fine — but check with your local composting facility to make sure. Note that these materials should not be put into a back yard compost bin as the temperature usually does not get hot enough to kill the disease or stop the seeds from sprouting.

December 12

Tool Thyme

Everyone had to bring a joke garden tool or accessory to the Christmas party potluck this year. We got the idea from that fabulous parody book called Smyth and Hawk'em by Tom Connor and Jim Downey (HarperPerennial, 1997).

Among our favorite tools were:

- a tiny dental instrument from Hilary (she's in dentistry school) for "weeding the middle path" during those times when you've veered too far off-center.

- an 11-foot fishing pole with a tiny spade attached for Mike — Mr. City Farmer, who has run our urban agriculture organization for 20 years but still wouldn't touch gardening with a ten-foot pole. Wes figured 11 feet might do it.

- a pair of designer jeans for Wes with a little patch of green shag carpet across the butt. So he can always cover his piles.

- A pith helmet and protective goggles, a must for all staff, so that when they open the shed, the stupid stick (that Wes stuffed into the crack to prevent the rain from getting in) doesn't fall on their heads and kill them. (The stick was removed shortly after the party.)

Cobbling Together a Garden Shed

How many corncobs does it take to build a cob house? If you are one of those people who think cob houses are constructed from corn cobs, let me assure you, not one kernel will be harmed in the construction of our cob garden shed.

I first learned about cob back in the last century, when I picked up a brochure on the Down to Earth Building Bee. This local non-profit group worked with a First Nations community in Bella Coola, B.C., to build a small meeting place. A series of workshops was held over three summers, drawing participants from diverse backgrounds eager to learn about this ancient, earth-friendly building method.

So what is cob, exactly? According to the Cob Cottage Company website, "the word cob comes from an Old English root meaning 'a lump or rounded mass'." A mixture of clay, sand, and straw is first stomped by foot into the right consistency, then scooped up by the handful and formed into lumps. The lumps are then used to sculpt self-supporting, load-bearing walls. This sustainable method of construction has been used for centuries in Western Europe. In England, you'll find cob houses up to 500 years old, still standing and still cozy and comfortable, despite the cool, damp climate. Its resistance to rain and cold makes cob well suited to Pacific Northwest climates. There are dozens of houses, cottages, barns, and studios up and down the west coast built of earthen materials. In Portland, Oregon, People's Food Co-op is building a new 6,000-square-foot (560-square-meter) store out of cob — the first permitted use of cob there in a commercially-zoned building. In fact, green architecture is enjoying a revival throughout North America.

Cob is just one example of earthen architecture; other methods include adobe (common in the U.S. Southwest), rammed earth, straw bale, and compressed earth bricks. Cob is the easiest approach to raw earth construction because you don't need wooden forms or any structural framing for wall construction. There's no need to build in straight lines. Cob dwellings are natural, organic, and free flowing. The material dries almost as hard as concrete, yet you can add on, cut out, or reshape at any time.

I thought it might be cool to have a cob structure in our garden, but then promptly forgot about it until our old wood tool shed rotted away last year. Mike piled Sharon and I into the car to go shopping for sheds at Home Depot. There they were — a whole parking lot full of bland, pre-fab, metal sheds, ready for the taking.

"A big box made of ugly metal, that should spruce up the joint," I said to Mike.

"We're an educational garden; what sort of message would this give to people?" Sharon lamented.

It was two against one, so we left empty-handed. But we needed a new shed and I didn't have an alternative solution, until a woman walked into the garden one day inquiring about cob. I dug out my old Down to Earth Building Bee brochure and the two of us got excited about cob. I presented my idea for a cob garden shed to Mike and Sharon the next day. Mike resisted, but once again, it was two against one.

"No new projects," Mike said. "I thought we agreed."

"Yes, but we always say that," Sharon said. "And then we take them on anyway."

Like most non-profits we're chronically overworked, understaffed, and subject to the fickle finger of funding.

"But how will we fund it?" he said, predictably.

"I don't know," I said. "Maybe we'll throw a giant fall fundraiser. We can sit around on straw bales and eat corn on the cob and cobbler. We can shoot cobs, play cobs and robbers, smoke cob pipes, cob for apples, and scary things up a bit with fire-eating cobbers," I said.

"Not bad," said Mike. "But where do we get the corn cobs to build this thing?"

Obviously, we needed some staff education before we went ahead. My research led me to landscape designer and green builder, John Freeman, of Erth Design Consultants. John has been involved in numerous green-building projects throughout B.C., including a cob garden shed for Lifecycles, an environmental group in Victoria, B.C.; a straw-bale structure for Camp Narnia at Shawnigan Lake on Vancouver Island; and an 1,800-square-foot (170-square-meter) cob house on Denman Island, several hours and a couple of ferry boat rides from Vancouver. John has also designed and built gardens throughout the Greater Vancouver area and on Vancouver Island. He topped up our scant cob education and lent us some books on the subject. We liked him because he laughed at our jokes and so we decided to sign him on as our project designer.

John encouraged us to visit the only cob structure in Vancouver — a small guest house built by the Down To Earth Building Bee crew in an East Vancouver back yard. The project brought about 70 people together in a creative and cooperative way, much like an old-fashioned barn raising. Ian Marcuse, the project coordinator, was there to meet us; it was his back yard so he didn't have too far to go.

The cob house was beautiful and looked like it had grown right up out of the forested garden. It was a fluid, curvy, 100-round-foot (nine-round-meter) structure, more sculpture than building. It had a granite foundation that rose up from the ground about a foot (about a third of a meter).

"This is essential in our rainy climes to protect the cob from excessive splash," said Ian.

The requisite two-foot (.66-meter) overhang, also for rain protection, was finished in polished red cedar, salvaged from a hot tub factory. A good "hat and boots" is what's required on the wet coast — a recommendation that must have slipped the minds of some conventional builders. You won't find any leaky cob-dos. A Mexican-style sun was sculpted right into the surface of the cob before the porous natural plaster was applied. Arched Romanesque windows were set into the foot-thick (.3-meter-thick) cob walls, creating deep knick-knack shelves inside. A little tile sign over the glass front doorway — Mi Casa es Su Casa — welcomed us.

As we stepped into the guest house, we saw a cob bed strewn with colorful pillows and Mexican blankets. The bed/couch was formed right out of the wall and stood on driftwood legs. Next to it was a side table, also extended from the wall with driftwood rising up out of it as a decorative armrest. The ceiling was lined with a lattice, row upon row of alder branches laid tightly together. And the floor looked like tile, but was actually rammed earth that had been oiled with linseed. Ian swept it while we were there to show us you could do so without losing the floor.

Cob is easy to learn and inexpensive to build. Marcuse spent about $1,300 on materials. He got clay from local building sites, unused straw bales from a racetrack, and sand from gravel pits. He told us he could mobilize his cob people quickly through the cob phone tree if we needed a crew. The people of the cob — I had entered a whole new world.

We came back to the garden excited. From that point on Mike became the Great Cob Crusader, talking up his brilliant idea at every opportunity. In addition to promoting our project, we began to scrounge materials and store them up in the Back 40, an enclosed area of our garden. What was once our outdoor class-room, with neat little beds teeming with lettuce and leeks, soon looked like a construction site.

Our mudpie garden shed would be the first public cob struc-ture in Vancouver. Now when visitors came in to find out about composting or rain barrels, they could also learn about earth-friendly building techniques and living roofs. They would see how beautiful, durable, and affordable it was and come to under-stand the low environmental impact of this sustainable building option. Aside from its educational value, the cob shed had a prac-tical side: it would house all our garden tools, push mowers, and wheelbarrows. Of course, this was going to take a little longer than just putting up a Home Depot special.

John drew up a preliminary design. The shed was to be tucked unobtrusively into a corner of our garden, facing out onto the driveway and back lane. At first it was too tall. Without get-ting a building permit, we were restricted to a ten foot-by-ten-foot (nine-square-meter) structure.

"This looks more like Cob Castle," Mike said to John. "What we need is more of a hobbit house. We can put a round door on it."

John went back to the drawing board and eventually we had a virtual rendering of the shed and a 3-D model. We may have to crawl into the shed on our hands and knees now, but at least it won't detract from the garden.

"It's not a hobbit house, it's a mouse house," I complained.

"You know," Mike said, ignoring me. "The Lord of the Rings movie is hot. This might be an opportunity for us,"

"Uh huh," I said skeptically.

"Hobbits for the Environment," he said. "Or hey, how about Wear Green for Tolkien!"

"Yeah, and I'll be the Hobbit Hotline Operator."

The environmentally friendly side of this building project appealed to us. After all, the cob building was completely com-postable! That is, unlike conventional building materials, the natural materials used to build cob could return to the earth without leaving a trace of chemicals. It's practically tree-free and doesn't depend on manufactured materials or energy-guzzling power tools. And because of the thick walls, cob has high thermal value and requires less energy to heat. Some cob buildings conserve even more energy by incorporating passive solar or geothermal heating systems. But of course what really sold us on the cob shed was that we could hide out there if the big one hits, a perennial concern for residents in this area of seismic activity.

"Cob buildings are historically very safe in earthquakes," John said. According to Cob Cottage, there are medieval earthen houses 13 stories high in a fault zone in South Yemen. And a cob mansion in New Zealand survived two major earthquakes while the surrounding town crumbled.

"Cob is more flexible than concrete block buildings because of the fibrous matrix formed by the straw," said John. And because a cob structure is essentially all one piece, there are no weak joint points. Cob is also fireproof and ideal for ovens, stoves, and chimneys.

From a health perspective, allergy sufferers will find relief from molds and mildews in cob structures. Because vapor barriers are not used, the walls can breathe and there is no moisture build-up. The non-toxic building materials mean no sick building syndrome, either. But earthen structures are not the only ones scoring environmental points on the green building front.

According to Environmental Building News, a bimonthly newsletter out of Vermont, "green building is a loosely defined collection of land-use, building design and construction strategies that reduces environmental impacts." A growing environmental consciousness in the building sector has resulted in exciting projects like the C.K. Choi Building on the University of British Columbia campus. This 30,000-square-foot (2,790-square-meter) building is made largely from recycled materials. There are compost toilets inside, rain barrels on the roof, a gray water system used for on-site irrigation, and carbon dioxide-hungry Gingko biloba trees lining the street outside the building. The best compliment the project manager had on opening day was that there was no "new building" smell. Other local developers are also using salvaged materials and adding eco-features such as geothermal heating and cooling systems, water-conserving sumps, permeable paving, and drought-tolerant gardens.

In August of 2001, the Greater Vancouver Regional District organized a conference called Green Buildings and Sustainable Communities. Among the attendees were officials, municipal staff, builders, developers, building owners and managers, architects, engineers, and non-governmental organizations. In plenary sessions and workshops, they learned about the latest ideas and practices in green-building design and green infrastructure. It appears to be a global trend. In September 2002, a Sustainable Building Conference was held in Oslo, Norway, attracting hundreds of delegates from all over the world. We decided to announce our own foray into green building at a promotional night on St. Patrick's Day.

In spite of the clear instructions on the flyers, Mike, John, and I were the only ones dressed as hobbits on March 17th. Wearing green velvet britches, a hood, and cloak, John gave an excellent slide show on green buildings from around the world. He explained that it is possible to learn how to build your own cob structure by taking this one-week workshop.

"Participants will learn how to select a site, choose materials, build a foundation, prepare a mix, and build a wall. We will also cover windows and doors, woodwork, floor materials, insulating issues, detail work, finishing, and some plastering," John said.

In reality, the cob building would be going on for the entire month of June (we pray for dry weather so we can build the optimum one-foot of height per day), but the one-week intensive was our workshop component. Hired professional cobbers, apprentices, volunteers, and weekend drop-ins would fill out the rest of the crew.

I served green tea while Mike filled them in on the green roof that would be installed atop the garden shed. "We'll plant wisteria, grasses, sedums, and other flora to provide beauty, but also to absorb rain water and for added insulation," he said. The Cob Crusader has already scraped some scruffy, weed-infested moss off a neighbor's roof in anticipation of the living roof. He's trying to keep it alive in the Back 40 without much cooperation from the staff.

Afterwards, I invited the guests to take a wee walk around the garden and a wee pee in our compost toilet if need be. With perks like that, we're sure to get all the sign-ups we need.

July 6

The Mad Shredder

I got back from lunch today and Wes, the Mad Shredder, was at it again. We haven't had to chop any yard waste since we got the small electric shredder. Wes looked up at me with a gleam in his eye.

"What are you doing," I screamed suddenly. "Those are my bamboo stakes!"

"I ran out of things to shred," Wes said in a jittery voice.

"Cut back on the caffeine, man, or I'll have to pull the plug on that grinder of yours," I said.

Contacts & Resources

GRASS

We maintain a list of local organic gardeners and landscapers on the City Farmer website, but check with your landscape and nursery organization to source them in your area. <www.city-farmer.org/orglandscape.html>

Groups/Organizations

B.C. Landscape and Nursery Association
#101-5830 176A St.
Surrey, BC V3S 4H5

Phone: (604) 574-7772 Fax: (604) 574-7773
E-mail: bclnainfo@telus.net
Website: <www.canadanursery.com/bclna>

Gaia Green Products Ltd.
9130 Granby Road
Grand Forks, BC V0H 1H1
Phone: (250) 442-3745 Fax: (250) 442-3749
Toll Free 1-800-545-3745
E-mail: gaiagreen@direct.ca
Website: <www.gaiagreen.ca>
In addition to making a great line of natural, slow-release organic fertilizers for the lawn and garden, Gaia is providing seminars and consultations for commercial landscapers and farmers to help them get off chemicals.

Cobra Head
W9545 Highway 18
Cambridge, WI 53523
Phone: (608) 423-9119 Fax: (608) 423-4884
E-mail: info@cobrahead.com
Website: <www.cobrahead.com>
Laura, our obsessive weeder, has given the thumbs-up to a couple of Cobra Head's tools. She likes the precision weeder and cultivator but she loves the flagstone and sidewalk crack weeder!

Organic Landscape Alliance
30 Duncan Street, Suite 201
Toronto, ON M5V 2C3
Phone: (416) 596-7989 Fax: (416) 596-0345
E-mail: info@organiclandscape.org
Website: <www.organiclandscape.org>

Seattle Public Utilities
Community Services Division
Resource Conservation Section
710 Second Ave, Suite 505

Seattle, WA 98104

Phone: (206) 684-7560

Website: <www.pcn.ci.seattle.wa.us>

Books/Publications/Magazines

How To Get Your Lawn and Garden Off Drugs, by Carol Rubin. Whitecap Books, 1989

Second Nature, by Michael Pollan. Dell Publishing, 1991

Six Steps to Natural Lawn Care. A brochure produced by the Greater Vancouver Regional District. It is in PDF format on their website <www.gvrd.bc.ca>

Lawns. Rodale Organic Gardening Basics, Rodale, 2000

The Lawn: A History of an American Obsession, by Virginia Scott Jenkins. Smithsonian Institution Press, 1994

The Chemical-Free Lawn, by Warren Schultz. Rodale Press, 1989

Ecologically Sound Lawn Care for the Pacific Northwest, by David K. McDonald. Seattle Public Utilities, 1999. Available as a PDF on the web: <www.ci.seattle.wa.us/util/lawncare/LawnReport.html> or E-mail david.mcdonald@ci.seattle.wa.us or phone (206)684-7560.

Natural Yard Care: Five Steps to Make Your Piece of the Planet a Healthier Place to Live, produced by King County, City of Seattle, and the Saving Water Partnership. First Edition, 2003. To order this excellent booklet, call the Natural Lawn and Garden Hotline (206) 633-0224.

The Blooming Lawn: Creating a Flower Meadow, by Yvette Verner. Chelsea Green, 1998

Websites

Evergreen Foundation. <www.evergreen.ca>
This group is busy greening school yards and play-grounds across the country.

Green Teacher. <www.greenteacher.com>
These guys promote school yard greening. You can order their magazine on-line.

Pesticides: Making the Right Choice for the Protection of Health and the Environment.
<www.parl.gc.ca/InfocomDoc/36/2/ENVI/Studies/Reports/envi01-e.html>
A recent Environment Canada study on pesticides in the urban environment.

Seattle Utilities, Grasscycling.
<www.ci.seattle.wa.us/util/lawncare/default.htm>
Seattle has led the way in home composting education since the mid-1980s; now they're at the forefront again with grasscycling.

GREEN BUILDING

Groups/Organizations

Erth Design Consultants
John Freeman
E-mail: erthdesign@shaw.ca
Website: <www.erth.ca>

The Down to Earth Building Bee
Ian Marcuse
1117 Salsbury Drive
Vancouver, BC V5L 4A9
Phone/Fax: (604) 253-6281
E-mail: dtebb@alternatives.com
Website: <www.alternatives.com/cob-building>

The Cob Cottage Company
Box 123
Cottage Grove, OR 97424
Phone/Fax: (541) 942-2005
Website: <www.deatech.com/cobcottage>
This company also has a newsletter called *The CobWeb.* You can subscribe on-line.

Books/Publications/Magazines

Buildings of Earth and Straw: Structural Design for Rammed Earth and Straw-Bale Architecture, by Bruce King. Ecological Design Press, 1996

Straw Bale Building: How to Plan, Design and Build With Straw, by Chris Magwood and Peter Mack. New Society Publishers, 2000

The Rammed Earth House, by David Easton and Cynthia Wright. Chelsea Green Publishing, 1996

The Cobber's Companion, by Michael G. Smith. Second Edition. Cob Cottage Company, 1998

Websites

Cobworks. <www.cobworks.com>
The Mayne Island, B.C., people of the cob.

Development Center for Appropriate Technology.
<www.dcat.net/index.php>
Some great suggested reading here:
< www.dcat.net/resources/reviews.php#straw>

Environmental Building News.
< www.buildinggreen.com>
A bi-monthly newsletter on environmentally sustainable design and construction.

Green Building Professionals Directory.

CHAPTER 5

Water Wisdom

August 17

The Wet Coast

We organized our first annual City Farmer picnic this month and got rained out. We still had it, but a picnic in a boardroom is a bit stuffy. Mike kept calling the picnic to order. This has been one of the wettest summers on record. In fact, the greenhouse has been leaking so badly we've taken to wearing umbrella hats. The torrential rains finally forced us to have the windows recaulked. Working in a greenhouse is not as glamorous as it seems — although it was exciting having two men splayed on glass over top of me.

The Water Wise Guys

Someone is peeing on the coastal strawberries in our street-front water-wise garden. They're all yellow. Such is the fate of the curbside urban garden. We've had people attacking the signs, running over the wood curbs, digging up the wood blocks in the pathway, and using the shrubby penstemon as a dog toilet. We've even spotted a few locals drinking out of our rain barrels, not exactly where I would want to be getting my eight glasses a day. Despite the occasional acts of vandalism, the garden has been a wonderful addition to our public demonstration garden. Now, just by strolling up the sidewalk, we can show visitors the principles of water-wise gardening. Of course, when the garden first opened we knew absolutely nothing about the subject, but experience has made us much wiser.

Our water-wise garden was officially opened in May of 1997. Ross Waddell, the garden designer and our resident native plant expert, commandeered the gala opening event along with Jeff Smyth, water conservation analyst for the city — our Water Wise Guys. Some of our honored guests would include the mayor, city engineers and planners, Parks Board officials, and neighborhood residents and businesses. Two school groups were also scheduled for workshops and the media were invited. To complicate matters, there was some kind of environmental conference going on in the building we share with several other groups (so we could not use the boardroom if it rained) and parking was at a premium. But the event was well-scheduled and we had a lot of staff stationed at key points around the site. As long as we stuck to the agenda, we'd be fine.

The crew of the nationally-broadcast television show *Canadian Gardener* arrived half an hour ahead of schedule — in fact, ahead of Julia, our media handler, throwing Mike into paroxysms of tai chi. I popped a few herbal tranquilizers and for some reason, Ross donned latex gloves. We all have our crutches. Let the operation begin.

Unfortunately, it didn't begin soon enough. A group of school children arrived for their water workshop, also ahead of schedule.

"Have you seen a guy with a tap on his head yet?" Ross asked me urgently.

"No," I said.

"He's supposed to do the workshop. Are you sure?" he asked.

"I think I would have noticed him," I said.

Ross ran off in search of Water Lily, the water department mascot, leaving the school children to run willy-nilly through the bed of woolly pussy toes.

David Tarrant, host of *Canadian Gardener*, cornered Mike as he was doing some tai chi in front of the newly installed rain barrels tucked away at the end of the driveway. When David casually asked him ON CAMERA how the rain barrel system worked, Mike replied, "Water goes in, water goes out."

And there you have it, ladies and gentleman, the Zen total of our knowledge on water conservation. You can all go home now. There is never a Water Wise Guy around when you need one.

Fortunately, this interview was cut short as Mike was nearly trampled to death by another group of school kids who actually arrived on time for their wormshop with Jan in the compost demonstration garden in the back of the building.

The mayor arrived late; in checked shirt and jeans he looked like a regular city farmer. Behind him was the guy with a tap on his head, followed by a mob of city engineers in suits looking like Wise Guys themselves. The media rushed in for the photo op. The mayor's parking spot was taken, so Mike had to double as a parking attendant. He drove the mayor's car around the neighborhood several times before finding a spot a few blocks away. This was not a bad thing, as it kept him out of the media spotlight. But Mike always was a sucker for a pretty face. Just as he returned, Oga Nwobosi from The Weather Network showed up and asked him sweetly, ON CAMERA, about the darling little plant with the white berries.

"Ballus whitus," Mike blurted out. "That would be the, uh, Latin name."

"Trailing snowberry, it's a trailing snowberry actually," said Ross. Finally, a Water Wise Guy to the rescue. "Now if you'll all join me in watching the children's water workshop."

And he steered them over to the gummy gooseberries where Water Lily was leading the children through a series of water activities and teaching them about the various forms of water. Camera shutters started clicking and tapes began to roll.

It was time for the official opening ceremony. Ross made his opening remarks in front of the nodding onions. "Two hundred years ago, Captain George Vancouver's ship, Discovery, sailed towards the home of the Coast Salish peoples — a land of towering coniferous trees, flowing streams, and leaping salmon. The city of Vancouver grew up in the midst of this coastal temperate rainforest where winters are typically cool and wet. Much of the forest and many of the streams that were originally here have since been lost. But the rain endures, and sometimes it seems it will never end," said Ross looking to the skies. Rain clouds were gathering overhead. Everyone laughed.

People were starting to pour out of the building. The environmentalists must be on a coffee break. But why were they carrying ropes? Everyone was a bit distracted by the sideshow.

"The Pacific Coast is not always wet," Ross continued. "Summers are often extremely dry and then one is reminded that water is an essential element of life. Homeowners often place great demands on the city water supply at these times. By tending the land in a more sensitive, water-conserving manner, Vancouverites can ensure that fresh water will continue to flow well into the future." Everyone clapped. Or was that thunder?

The environmentalists were congregating on the railway tracks right beside the water-wise garden as Jeff Smyth stepped to the podium. Well, there was no podium, but he was speaking. Everyone was still listening. I felt a rain drop on my cheek.

"During the summer, up to 40 per cent of the water used in Vancouver is for outdoor watering," said this Water Wise Guy, "despite annual lawn-sprinkling regulations, which come into effect June first. The pressure on our valuable water resource will only increase as the regional population grows," Jeff said.

The environmentalists were beginning to lie down on the railway tracks and we had begun to lose our audience. It was sprinkling now.

Jeff braved the elements. "This unique water conservation garden was developed by the City of Vancouver, in cooperation with City Farmer to demonstrate the principles of water-wise gardening. In addition to the garden, we are offering subsidized rain barrels, public and school education programs, a water conservation hotline, and information available in print and on our website."

Most of the cameras were now focused on the railway tracks, their lenses splattered with raindrops.

Ross jumped in to save the day. He began to plant up some white fawn lilies, hoping to win back audience attention with interesting activities. "We have used native, drought-tolerant plants in the garden and designed it to reduce water consumption in the dry summer periods and reduce run-off during the rainy season," he said.

He demonstrated the use of the rain barrel, filling a watering can and watering the plants with the rain water. As fascinating as that was, it was no match for what was happening just beyond the leafy kinnikinnick.

The "eco-warriors in training" were now tying themselves to the railway tracks, giving a whole new meaning to railway ties. This, of course, makes for much better television, but a rather nerve-wracking tour. I popped another herbal tranquilizer, Mike's tai chi affliction was back, and Ross snapped his latex gloves in frustration.

"By following the principles of water-wise gardening, contouring of the ground, soil conditioning using compost, collecting rain water in barrels, and using native plants that are naturally adapted to dry conditions, we can dramatically reduce water consumption." Ross was almost shouting now to be heard over the thunder. But no one was listening.

The lightening made for interesting effects and The Weather Network was in its glory. But the kids had already scampered back to school and Mike scurried off to get the mayor's car. Even the eco-warriors had called it a day. We were losing our audience.

In a moment of desperation and wild abandon, I lured the damp engineers up the driveway and into the back garden with the promise of a flower that smelled purple. So there they were, the City Wise Guys, stooped over a giant Florentine iris, ties dangling in the dirt, inhaling deeply. Yes, they agreed, it does smell purple. I considered it an engineering feat, moving left-brainers to a right-brained activity. I passed out some umbrellas. For the moment, the tour could continue, albeit without the media. But just a word to the wise: water conservation is a hard sell in a downpour.

Hot Tips

PRINCIPLES OF ECOLOGICAL LANDSCAPING
By Ross Waddell, M.E.S.
Prepared for the City of Vancouver Waterworks Design Branch

Follow the Land by watching the rain as it falls onto it. The contours of the land can be changed to catch the rain water and speed or slow its flow, holding it in the ground for use by plants.

Care for the Soil by adding compost or decomposed organic matter. Compost helps the soil hold water and adds nutrients needed for plant growth. Mulches prevent the soil from overheating and drying out.

Gather the Rain by catching it in rain barrels when it falls and holding it for later use. The rain water costs nothing and it can be used in the garden during the summer when the ground is dry.

Plant Naturally by layering plants to make shade and using species that are native to this land. Native plants are naturally rain-watered and are mostly adapted to wet winter and drier summer conditions.

Water Wisely with a gentle hand and simple tools such as a soaker hose that slowly and softly drips water into the ground. Plants adapted to dry summers do not need much water a few years after planting.

Tend Patiently with a sparing hand, keeping in mind that plants will grow larger. Plants use nutrients found naturally in the soil and in the added compost. They do not need man-made chemicals to make them grow better.

Spread the Seeds by sharing the fruits of the garden within the community. Developing wisdom of the land insures that the city will be a healthy one with food and water for all.

February 9

Celestine Prophetics

Mike and Ross called each other with similar news on a water-wise project they're working on together. When Ross commented on the synchronicity, Mike said, "Well, that's how we communicate around here — telepathetically."

Yup, we're pretty pathetic all right.

Water Wars

"A United Nations study has concluded that water will be the oil of the 21st Century. The World Bank predicts that wars will be fought over fresh water."

I was reading the opening lines in a press release for *Captured Rain*, a television documentary about fresh water, free trade, and the looming crisis in North America. Hell, the war on water has already been declared and it's being fought in our tiny little demonstration garden.

Some time ago, I began to suspect that Sharon was over-watering the garden. Mike, the city farmer who hadn't gardened a day in his life, was convinced she was under-watering. And of course Sharon was certain her watering was just right. But Mama Bear (my code name) is determined to show Papa and Baby that they are wrong, wrong, wrong. This is not the first time water wars have been waged at the garden. Mind you, it's always been a civil war and we use purely non-violent means.

I first had the soaker hoses installed back in the long hot summer of '98. After standing for hours every day watering my fool head off (while Wes was on holidays as usual), I sent our summer gardener, Megan, to buy soaker hoses for the tomatoes, peppers, and beans and a new watering wand that didn't completely drench the right side of my body. Wes had been resisting this "modernization," so I had to stage this water coup while he was away.

Megan was a seasoned horticulturist. She'd had specialized irrigation training in a remote semi-desert camp. She could deploy soaker hoses with precision and touch them off with a deft quarter-turn twist of the wrist. She taught me well.

"Just make them sweat," she told me over and over, until I was repeating the mantra in my sleep. "Otherwise, there will be too much pressure and the tiny hose holes will burst wide open."

Back then we used to leave the hoses on for six hours at a time and water about every three days. The garden flourished.

"We've never been able to grow cucumbers before," I said to Megan. Usually we get too much moisture and not enough heat out here on the coast. But all that summer, we delivered bushel baskets of gorgeous cucumbers along with other vegetables, herbs, fruits, and flowers to our friends at May's Place, a downtown eastside hospice. But this year, we were in a real pickle.

"The cucumbers look like drowned gherkins," I said ever so tactfully.

"They *are* gherkins," said Sharon, "for pickling."

"Still, do you really think we should leave the water on all the time?" I asked, softening my approach.

"Yes," said Sharon standing her ground.

"This is not water conservation," I protested. "This is waterloggery."

"You've been brainwashed," said Sharon defensively.

I decided to take another tack and broach the subject of sweating soaker hoses. Sharon didn't just turn the hoses on: she detonated them. Her heavy-handed technique set off water explosions all over the garden; it was like walking through a minefield. You never knew when you might be hit by a burst of waterfire.

"Propaganda!" Sharon exclaimed. "Look at the harvests we're getting. They've never been more abundant."

Okay, so the tomatoes were plump and the peppers were perky, but those cukes were scrawny.

"And remember, every crop has good years and bad years," Sharon said.

"I still think the soil looks dry," said Mike, the guy who wouldn't stick his finger in the dirt if his life depended on it.

"Do the finger test," Wes would always say to me. He'd stoop down and stick his forefinger about two inches into the ground: if the soil was moist, no need to water. I've used the finger test ever since, even at home where I maintain the grounds for the owner. This year, I stopped watering by the end of September, but my landlord vetoed me. Unbeknownst to me he'd had me under surveillance.

"The rhodos are wilting," he said accusingly when he showed up on my doorstep. So, out came the sprinkler.

My next door neighbor, with nary a plant or patch of lawn in his yard, was watching me. "You're not going to water at this time of year, are you?" he said accusingly. Everyone has an opinion on how much water is enough.

As for the rest of the staff, they were neither with me nor against me, wisely opting for neutral positions amid the warring factions. I sent one of our part-timers off on a reconnaissance mission. Isabelle (my mole) was to gather vital information at an irrigation workshop out in Delta. I was building my case.

"Give Mama Bear all you've got," I said to her when she returned.

"There is no surefire strategy," she said. "Perennials should be allowed to dry out between waterings or they will rot, but vegetables should be kept watered. The amount of watering depends on the type of soil and the weather."

I read through the rest of her report. Turning on the soaker hose too high will make it spray like a sprinkler and unnecessary evaporation will occur. Turn the hose on until it sweats, one-quarter turn only. Aha! Proof. Experiment by leaving the hose on for a period of time and then digging a hole to see how deep it watered. The goal is to have healthy plants while using as little water as possible. Okay, now I had some ammunition. The troops would have to tow the hose from now on. The war was over, or so I thought.

You might be wondering why we were all so feverish about water conservation — I mean, we're a compost demonstration garden, for mercy's sake. The conversion started slowly. At first we just followed general organic gardening principles. Research shows that organically grown plants are healthier and more vigorous than those grown in unimproved or chemically dependent soil are. They develop stronger root systems that make them more drought-tolerant. So we added our home-grown compost to the food beds to help increase the water-holding capacity of the soil. We also mulched them with a thick layer of leaves, grass clippings, or straw to block weed growth and hold moisture. And we also sowed green manures like red clover or winter rye in the late summer, to retain moisture and to hold the soil in place during the winter.

But it wasn't until we forged an alliance with the city water department and jointly planted a water-wise garden a few years ago that we were forced to become more water-aware. Since that time, we've taken more serious water conservation measures in the garden. We collect water in our rain barrels; the overflow from one of them runs into a perforated sump that allows water to slowly percolate into the ground. We practice natural lawn care on a neighbor's boulevard, leaving the clippings on the lawn to add moisture. The only time the lawn or the water-wise garden gets a drink is when it rains. Our compost toilet uses no water to flush, saves thousands of gallons of water every year, and produces no sewage. We even had another irrigation system installed in a perennial bed. The smart regulators "sense" when the plants need a drink and deliver water directly to the root zone. Both the drip irrigation system and the soaker hoses encourage deep root growth, help reduce evaporation and run-off, and keep foliage dry, preventing mildew-related diseases.

We all vowed to stop our wasteful water practices on the home front, too, and enlisted family members. We would not leave the tap running when we brushed our teeth, or flush unnecessarily. It did seem a waste that we were using drinking water to flush our own waste. We would take shorter showers and only run full dishwasher loads. And when it came to garburetors, we all resolved: Just Don't Do It. According to experts, not only are you wasting good drinking water, but you are also taxing the sewer system with the food waste and washing away a valuable resource that could be composted and turned into fertilizer for the garden. We were so immersed in our new ideology that it was inevitable that one of us would become an extremist.

A certain member of our gang (who wishes to remain anonymous) has taken his war on water to the streets. This self-appointed water vigilante combs the neighborhood looking for water wasters and their weapons of mass destruction: sprinklers run amok, hoses without spring-loaded nozzles, and leaky taps. You'd be wise to be more water wary with this water warrior on the prowl. If he finds you watering the sidewalk, he'll kick over your sprinkler. Hose down your driveway instead of sweeping it and you'll hear his war cry: "There's 450 million people on the planet facing water shortages and you're washing the driveway with drinking water!" Water your lawn on the wrong day and you'll get a warning. Violate the sprinkling regulations again and you'll be reported to the water conservation hotline. Wash your car excessively or splash too exuberantly in your wading pool or hot tub and you could wind up as the poster criminal for the war on water.

In a region where scarecrows wear wetsuits, is this kind of water fascism really warranted? The problem in the Greater Vancouver Regional District (GVRD) is that 70% of our rain falls in autumn and winter. We use over 260 million gallons (one billion liters) of water each day; during the summer when lawns and gardens are being watered, that consumption can double. The storage capacity in our three watersheds is limited and as our population increases, the demand for water also increases. By conserving water, we help reduce the need for expanded facilities and costly upgrades to our water system. Granted, for us water scarcity is just a matter of economics. The water is there if we need it; we just have to pay for it. Drought-stressed places like California, Arizona, and Nevada don't have that luxury. Nevertheless, we shouldn't be complacent. The wet coast has also felt the dry fingers of drought around its green little neck.

In October of 2002, GVRD watershed levels fell to near-crisis levels. The rains finally came, but we were only a few weeks away from mud milkshakes on tap. The summer before was even worse for some cities in the Pacific Northwest. Despite progressive water conservation policy, Washington State declared a water state of emergency. And over on Vancouver Island, B.C.'s capital city imposed stage-three water restrictions: Victoria residents were limited to drip or micro-spray irrigation systems. Sprinklers and even soaker hoses were banned. Hoses were permitted, but only with spring-loaded nozzles for watering shrubs, flowers, and veggie gardens. Hand watering was okay, but lawn watering was verboten.

"So what did you tell people to do during the water crisis?" I asked Geoff Johnson, the site educator at the Greater Victoria Compost Education Center.

"Our focus at the center was on mulching, composting, and encouraging people to switch their gardens from annual to perennial, as well as minimizing their lawn area and planting more drought-resistant native plants or food."

"How did people manage?" I asked.

"Quite well," Geoff said. "Some people were very creative."

As Geoff toured around the city, he saw xeriscaped (low-water, low-maintenance) gardens and good water-zoning (locating plants with similar needs for water and light near each other). Rain barrels were being used, too, but because Victoria has no rain barrel program, some of the systems were quite crude and inventive. He saw signs on properties where people were watering from wells. Some gardeners submerged gallon pots to allow water to filter down to plant roots. Geoff also mentioned a water injection system he saw in one yard; it had an attachment on the hose that injected water right to the root zone.

"Some people reused their bath water, too; some had permanent siphons on the taps," said Geoff. "One guy was throwing bath water out the bathroom window onto the roof where it then drained into his rain barrel system."

Gray water is the water that comes from the bath, shower, washing machine, or bathroom sink — a valuable resource for agriculture, horticulture, and home gardeners. Unfortunately, gray water systems are illegal in most cities. Not so in California, though. In 1992, gray water use was legalized there to help with the devastating effects of the drought.

And then there were those crazy Victorians who were painting their lawns green.

"Yeah, we're a little embarrassed about that," said Geoff.

Homeowners were having their lawns spray-painted with a water-soluble pigment to uphold their "garden city" status. We thought such illusions could only be found in Vegas where the lawns outside the grand casinos are ever emerald and the fountains flow profusely.

But even in the desert, the mirage is fading under water pressure. In 2001, the drought situation there got so bad that the Southern Nevada Water Authority started offering cash to any resident who would rip up their water-hungry lawns and replace them with native, drought-tolerant plantings. Homeowners were paid 40 cents a square foot ($3.60 per square meter) up to a maximum of $1,000. You can buy a lot of succulents for a grand. Other states like New Mexico, California, and Arizona are also gambling on financial-incentive plans to save water. Even retailers are jumping into water issues. In New York, an ecologically minded florist is responding to public water-guilt by creating drought-tolerant wedding bouquets, comprised mainly of succulents.

Water conservation has become public policy in Washington State, thanks to the Water Conservation Coalition of Puget Sound. Comprised of city and county government water authorities, the group has initiated water conservation demonstration gardens, education courses, and materials. Many ecological landscaping projects in the region promote water conservation: for example, by capturing rain water on site, as they do at the Garden of Eatin' and at Growing Vine Street in downtown Seattle. Some gardens, like the Broadview Superblock, do away with curbs and gutters to channel rain water over grassy swales, allowing the water to be absorbed back into the ground.

Seattle has also had residential water metering since the early 1900s. Consumption there is around 114 gallons (428 liters) per person per day compared to 155 gallons (582 liters) for the GVRD area where residential users account for more than half of the total regional consumption. There is ample evidence to show that when people have to pay directly for the water they use, their consumption drops. When water meters were introduced in Vernon, B.C., for example, consumption dropped by 16 percent. Victoria has had meters for decades and they use about 15 percent less water than Vancouver residents do. There are significant up-front costs with installing water meters, but when people get hit in the pocket book, they seem more willing to change their wasteful ways. And in the words of the water vigilante, "Water hogs should pay for their piggishness!"

Speaking of water hogs, Baby Bear was still trying to convince us she was ju-u-ust right.

Sharon marched into the greenhouse. She brandished a giant sunflower at us menacingly. "I knew we should have kept watering through October. Look at these roots, the soil is dry six inches down," she said.

"I told you the soil was dry," said Papa Bear.

"I told you so. I told you so," I mocked him. It was baby bear-ish, I know. Mike glared at me. "That's only because we haven't watered for a month and it only just started raining," I growled. Will the war never end?

"Let's try to put our irrigation differences aside, at least for the winter," said Mike.

He was right. Next spring the hoses will come out of hibernation and hopefully by then, the three bears will have a peacekeeping strategy. When these water crises arise, a more metered response is required.

"It's time to put our money where our mouth is," Mike said the next day. He pulled a car part out of his brief case.

"You got us a carburetor?" I said incredulously.

"It's a water meter," said Mike.

"But it's winter," I said. "Our water has been turned off."

"Yes," said Mike, "So we'll have a '00' reading on the meter between November and March."

"But that's cheating, isn't it?" I asked.

"Never mind that, where do we put the thing?" Mike said.

"If we put it on the tap at the side of the greenhouse, visitors won't be able to see it," said Sharon.

"We need to redo the porch, anyway," I said. "So let's tear it down and build our dream verandah, with storage cupboards and two sets of stairs. We can sit out there in the summer and sip mint juleps."

"It looks like I should have you on a meter," Mike said.

I metered my response. Hey, this thing was already working! "Then we can extend the tap from the wall and build a kind of display case for the water meter. We can shine a spotlight on it even. What do you think?" I said.

"Let me see if I've got this right," said Mike. "We save gallons of water, but spend buckets of money."

"That sounds ju-u-u-u-u-ust about right," said Baby Bear.

Hot Facts

BLUE GOLD FEVER

Canada is a water-rich country. Thar's Blue Gold in thar rivers and many thirsty folks would like to share in our bounty. We hold 20 percent of the world's fresh water. But — before you grab a bucket and stake your claim — we have only seven percent of the world's renewable fresh water supply, compared to Brazil at 18 percent, China at nine percent, and the U.S. at eight percent. [Source: Environment Canada Website: <www.ec.gc.ca/water/en/nature/prop/e_magic.htm> The Nature of Our Water. (Updated June 18, 2002)]

August 12

Well-seasoned Help

I've been leafing through our photo albums and Mike seems

to have a bit of a hiring theme happening. Way back in 1993, there's a shot of Chris Summerfield working out in the medicinal herb garden she designed, while Meadoe is teaching a wormshop in the worm corner . Skip ahead to '96 and there's Laura Plant potting up some pansies on the picnic table. And as always, past, present, and future, Spring is on the hotline. I'll bet Rain is in the forecast.

Twice Bitten

I had malaria on my mind as I walked in to the garden that morning. Barry and I were going to Belize for Christmas and we were learning about all the exotic diseases we could contract, including malaria, hepatitis A, dengue fever, and typhoid. We were debating on which pills to take and what shots to get, and all that research was putting a bit of a damper on the holiday.

"I think there are mosquitoes breeding in our sump," Mike said as he greeted me in the driveway.

"Terrific, why travel when you can catch an exotic disease in your own back yard?" I said.

"That's all we need, a West Nile Virus scare," Mike said.

"Let's have a look." I peered into the perforated sump, a big open cement pit designed to take storm water overflow from the downspout and let it slowly percolate into the ground. "Hmmm, standing water," I said. "An ideal breeding ground for mosquitoes." Oh, I was up on mosquitoes all right.

"You think?" Mike asked anxiously.

I stooped to take a closer look. There did seem to be some squiggly bits in there, probably just leaf fragments. "Organic debris," I said to Mike.

"But they're swimming," he said.

"It's the wind," I countered.

"You'd better steer clear of here on the tour this morning," he said. "Just in case."

"They'd have to be blind as bats to miss the sump," I said.

"We'll get Sharon on it as soon as she gets here," Mike said. "She'll know what to do."

I was meeting with staff from the city streets department on the "country lane" pilot project this morning. Our garden had been selected as one of three sites for a demonstration of a sustainable back lane. The lane is designed to allow rain water to absorb naturally into the ground, reducing the amount of storm water that is discharged into the sewer system. I was planning to give them the water conservation tour of the garden; the sump is smack in the middle of our water-wise garden and one of the rain barrels is piped to overflow into it.

When Sharon drove up, we hustled her to the sump. Sure enough, she confirmed the squiggly bits were mosquito larvae.

"I've got just the fix," Sharon said and ran into the greenhouse. She came back out carrying a bottle of biodegradable dish soap. She put a few drops into the sump water. "The soap will clog the breathing holes of the mosquito larvae," Sharon said. "A few drops of cooking oil would work, too."

Okay, situation normal, just as the city guys pulled in. We inspected the back lane with Deepak and Wilf. Our lane, which is short and has never been paved, leads up to our soon-to-be-constructed cob garden shed. I explained that the shed's "living roof" will be planted with grasses and succulents to promote natural water absorption. As we were reviewing the details of the project, I heard a high-pitched buzzing in my ear. I slapped myself on the side of the face. I missed and the mosquito bit the other cheek.

"Mosquito, huh? Hope it's not the West Nile kind," Wilf joked.

"Malaria would be worse," I said, not joking.

We returned to our discussion. Traditionally, when back lanes are paved, the asphalt extends their full width. Recently, the city has also provided partial-width paving. While these options provide a long-lasting driving surface, the storm water run-off from these lanes may pollute streams and contribute to sewage overflows during heavy rains. The country lane concept increases the area available for rain water to be absorbed. Allowing more water to drain into the ground recharges the water tables and in turn increases creek flows and enhances fish habitat.

Our country lane will have two narrow bands of hard surface running the length of the lane that will serve as wheel paths. The area between the bands will be structurally reinforced to support vehicles, then planted with grass. Permeable paving stones will be placed outside the bands and will butt up to our neighbor's property lines. Vegetation can grow in the spaces between the pavers to allow for rain water absorption. Project coordinators believe that a sustainable lane like this one will give neighborhoods a more attractive, greener, aesthetic, while reducing environmental impact and discharge into the city's storm sewer system.

There was another high-pitched whine in my ear. This time I got bit on the arm.

"Call out the swat team," said Deepak.

"Those mosquitoes really like you," said Wilf.

There was nothing wrong with their eyesight. "Oh yeah, I'm as plump and juicy as an Okanagan peach," I said.

"You've sure got a lot of mosquitoes around here," said Deepak.

"Yeah, one of the neighbors must have standing water in their yard," I said. "We'll have to get after them. Which reminds me, you haven't seen our compost toilet. It uses no water at all." Yup, gazing into a waterless toilet bowl was sure to get their minds off mosquitoes.

Back lanes are only drops in the bucket when it comes to impermeable surfaces. Fresh land is being gobbled up by high rises, big box stores, parking lots, and driveways; the more we pave and roof over, the more we threaten our natural water supplies. Conversely, the more green space we have, the better able we are to sustain agriculture and a growing population.

"If we look at the way we are paving the planet," said Deepak, "we begin to understand the connection between drought and urban sprawl."

According to a recent report prepared by American Rivers, the Natural Resources Defense Council, and Smart Growth America (see *Paving Our Way to Water Shortages* under Websites in Contacts and Resources at the end of this chapter), low rainfall and searingly hot summers aren't the only culprits on the drought front. The authors also point the finger at urban sprawl as a major contributing factor. They looked at impervious surfaces built between 1982 and 1997 in several U.S. cities. In greater Atlanta, nearly 213,000 acres (85,000 hectares) of land were paved or roofed over. That means that 132 billion gallons (495 billion liters) of rain water can no longer seep naturally back into the ground, to water trees, replenish aquifers, and filter back into rivers, streams, and lakes. Boston and its outlying areas are losing up to 102 billion gallons (382.5 billion liters) a year. The figure is 55 billion gallons (206 billion liters) in Washington, DC, close to 30 billion gallons (112 billion liters) in Houston, and almost 25 billion gallons (94 billion liters) in Seattle. A billion gallons (3.75 billion liters) of water can quench the daily needs of 27,500 people. Instead, that water falls onto an impervious surface and is diverted into storm drains.

It's not all bad news; many cities are making great strides in reducing storm water loss. Atlanta and Dallas-Fort Worth actually reclaim their storm water. Many North American cities, including Vancouver, B.C., and Chicago, IL, have downspout disconnect programs in place through which residents are encouraged to disconnect their residential roof downspouts to prevent them from feeding into the storm drains, and to redirect the water away from the house into a rock pit, the landscape, or into a rain barrel.

According to the city of Chicago's website, "Approximately 29,000 gallons (108,750 liters) of rain water drains each year from the roof of an average single family home in Chicago (estimated roof area 350 square feet or 32.6 square meters). In an intense Chicago storm (e.g., 1.8 inches of rain per hour or 4.5 centimeters per hour), a roof can drain approximately 24 gallons (90 liters) of rain water per minute. By comparison, the average kitchen faucet flows at about 2.5 gallons (9.38 liters) per minute."

Not only do downspout disconnect programs help offset the amount of tap water used for lawns and gardens, but they also help to prevent floods during severe rainstorms. Many cities are susceptible to flooding because the sewer system is still combined (storm water and sanitary sewage flow together in one pipe). In severe storms, sewage and storm water back up through household plumbing fixtures. This problem is compounded by the reduction in greenspace and the increased run-off.

"Drought has done wonders for rain barrel sales," I said. We were showing Wilf and Deepak the rain barrels in the back garden, avoiding the mosquito-infested sump in the front. The city of Vancouver has been offering subsidized rain barrels for several years now.

The unique half-barrel design fits snug against a wall, measures just under two feet by four feet (60 cm x 120 cm) at the base and stands 4.5 feet (135 cm) high. It is made of dark forest-green recycled plastic and holds 90 gallons (338 liters) of rain water. A plastic mesh screen at the top keeps out leaves and other large objects (like raccoons and squirrels!). It has a tap for a watering can and a tap near the base to attach a hose. If placed on a grade, water can be gravity fed through the hose to thirsty plants. Plants thrive on the soft, non-chlorinated water and the temperature doesn't shock them the way ice-cold water from the tap can. Rain barrel water is not potable, as certain roofing materials can leach chemicals into it, so don't let your spouse or pet drink from it. Designed by a city engineer, the Vancouver barrel is now being marketed to other municipalities and cities by a company called Rain Pail.

I spouted off some water facts to the city guys. "Assuming each home uses one 90-gallon (338-liter) barrel, water savings for each household would be around 1,300 gallons (4875 liters) in the peak demand summer months, or about one percent of summer household consumption."

Many other cities are also rolling out the barrel in response to parched lawns and dying vegetable patches. In Olympia, Washington, city officials sold all 278 rain barrels in a few hours. In Florida, many counties are offering workshops on how to make a rain barrel by adding spigots and screens to an old plastic drum. Clean plastic garbage cans and food-grade containers work well, too.

"Our water at the garden is shut off from November through March every year and we rely solely on the five rain barrels we have around the garden for hand-watering, washing garden tools and hands," I said.

"Where are the other barrels?" Deepak wanted to know.

"Oh, around the garden, here and there," I said casually. "You've seen one, you've seen them all."

"What about mosquitoes?" Wilf asked.

"What about mosquitoes?" I scratched nervously at the red welt on my arm.

"Well, I heard that one of the species of mosquitoes that carry West Nile virus really likes a rain barrel situation rather than an open water one."

"Really?" I said, my voice strained.

"You should probably put some mosquito screening over that opening instead of that plastic mesh," said Deepak.

"Good idea!" I said.

"Okay, so have you got more to show us?" asked Wilf.

"Not really, no, we're about done here, I think," I said.

After the city guys left, I decided to do some research on West Nile Virus (WNV). According to the centers for disease control in both Canada and the U.S., WNV is a mosquito-borne virus, normally passed between mosquitoes and birds. (Birds such as crows, ravens, magpies, and blue jays are susceptible to the virus.) WNV is transmitted to humans through the bite of an infected mosquito. Most people infected with WNV show no symptoms or have only mild flu-like symptoms lasting a week or less. In rare cases, however, WNV can cause meningitis or encephalitis.

Containers with standing water are favorite breeding grounds for mosquitoes that may be carrying WNV. Such containers include, pool covers, flower pots, pet bowls, wading pools, old tires, birdbaths, and rain barrels.

I called our local Rain Pail retailer to get her take on the rain barrel/mosquito issue. Megan told me that she'd heard Winnipeg was about to ban rain barrels.

"Well, of course, they have mosquitoes the size of chickens there," I said. "They're like West Nile Virus storage vats."

But when I followed up, I discovered that city officials were only insisting that mosquito screening cover any openings on the rain barrels and that the area around the downspout be tightly sealed. Another suggestion was to put a zinc source in contact with the water. Zinc discourages growth of fungi, bacteria, algae, and insects. A few galvanized nails should do the trick.

There are now positive human cases of WNV in both Canada and the U.S. and some deaths have occurred. Those most at risk are over 50 years of age, the very young, and those with immune-suppressed illnesses. Okay, so Mike and Sharon would probably succumb first. Then again, they hadn't been bitten — twice.

I was worn out when I got home that night.

"We made it through infectious disease day at the garden without being shut down by the health department," I told Barry.

"Come on, we're going shopping," he said.

"I'm too tired," I said. "I think I may have sleeping sickness."

"Come on," said Mr. Empathy. "This store will really perk you up. It's the Costco of Chinatown," he said.

As we walked into Big Lucky, my skin started to crawl. "How could you bring me here?" Barry loves seedy little finds. "You know I'm a Capers girl," I whined. (Capers is my favorite organic food store. I love their immaculate aisles and pristine bulk food bins, the artistic displays of sparkling clean fruits and colorful vegetables and the scrubbed faces of their perky staff.)

Big Lucky was not Capers. The floors were grimy. There were no aisles, only boxes and boxes of goods strewn haphazardly about the store. You had to fish things out yourself. There were no signs, no price tags. I began to feel flu-like symptoms.

"Get me out of this rat haven," I said to Barry who was happily rummaging through a crate of soya sauce. "We'll probably catch Bubonic plague in here." That is, if the mosquitoes at the garden didn't drive me batty first.

"I've got the perfect solution for mosquito control," said Sharon the next day at the garden. "Bats," she said and dumped a bat house and some literature on to my desk.

"Bats? You've got bats in the belfry if you think I'm going to have those little vampires flying around sucking my blood. I'm giving enough to the mosquitoes," I said.

"We don't have vampire bats here," said Sharon, calmly. She was used to my outbursts. "Even Martha Stewart rates bats as top insect controllers in the garden," said Sharon slyly.

Martha Stewart was so neat and clean. I relented, a little. "How can bats find mosquitoes? Aren't they blind?" I asked.

"They navigate using sophisticated ultrasonic signals. And it's a myth that they're blind," she said.

"Don't they carry rabies?" I said.

"Only about one half of one per cent." Sharon had done her homework.

"It's just the thought of them getting their dirty little claws in my hair," I said.

"When are you ever here at night," said Sharon.

"Let me have a look at the brochure," I said.

Holy West Nile Virus, bats can eat 3,000 mosquitoes a night! There are 16 species of these nocturnal critters in the Greater Vancouver area; the most common one is the brown bat. They are the only major predators of night-flying insects, according to Wild Birds Unlimited, our local bird store. They also pollinate fruit flowers and disperse seeds in tropical rainforests, aiding in reforestation. And the guano (bat poo) is an excellent fertilizer for the garden, too.

"Oh oh!" I said to Sharon as I read more of the bat literature. "Along with birds, horses, cats, domestic rabbits, chipmunks, gray squirrels, and striped skunks, bats have also been known to carry West Nile Virus. Well, that settles it, we can't risk it," I said.

A week later Capers had an outbreak of hepatitis A. Needless to say, Barry and I are doing a lot more of our shopping at Big Lucky now. As for Sharon, she hung the bat house in the garden that very day.

Hot Facts

SWALLOW THIS!

Dirk, the mosquito guy at the Fraser Valley Regional District, confirms that bats can get WNV, but like us they are known as "end hosts" — meaning it is unlikely there is enough of the virus in our blood for a mosquito to contract it from us. So bats and humans can get the virus, but probably won't be able to pass it on.

According to Dirk, bats are only a small part of a good mosquito-control initiative. They will only get some of the night-time mosquitoes, and not the daytimers. Swallows may actually be a better bet for mosquito control, especially if you're not fond of bats. They like to eat both daytime and early evening mosquitoes. So put up a swallow box this spring. Better yet, put up both.

November 14

Measuring Mercury

We've been shopping at Lee Valley Tools again. This time we stocked up on water toys for Mike to play with all winter long. We got a recoiling Rain Drain. The vinyl tube fits onto the bottom of your downspout and when it rains, the water pressure rolls it out so it can sprinkle your lawn or garden! Then, when it stops raining, it rolls back up all by itself! Mike will get hours of enjoyment out of watching that baby. We also got an electronic rain gauge and a new thermometer. Mike says we're going to start measuring everything in the garden — heart rate and blood pressure are next.

We had just put up the new thermometer outside when Mike found an old one lying around the greenhouse. "We didn't need a new thermometer, we already had one," he said.

"It's old, the mercury is probably gone," I said.

"Mercury never dies," replied Mike.

"Right," I said, "it just goes into retrograde."

Contacts and Resources

WATER

Groups/Organizations

Oasis Design
5 San Marcos Trout Club
Santa Barbara, CA 93105-9726
Phone: (805) 967-9956 Fax: (805) 967-3229
Website: <www.oasisdesign.net>
Oasis publishes and distributes books on water
technology.

Lee Valley Tools
1090 Morrison Drive
Ottawa, ON K2H 1C2
Phone: (613) 596-0350 Fax: (613) 596-3073
E-mail: customerservice@leevalley.com
Website: <www.leevalley.com>
You can probably tell how much we love our local
Lee Valley Tools store. They sell very cool gardening
gadgets.

Native Plant Society of British Columbia (NPSBC)
2012 William Street
Vancouver BC V5L 2X6
Phone: (604) 255-5719 Fax: (604) 258-0201
E-mail: information@npsbc.org
Website: <www.npsbc.org>
There is also a list of native plant nurseries at:
<www.npsbc.org/Education/NativePlantSale2001.pdf>

University of British Columbia
Botanical Garden
6804 SW Marine Drive
Vancouver, BC V6T 1Z4
Phone: (604) 822-3928 Fax: (604) 822-2016
Information Line (recorded): (604)822-9666
E-mail: botg@interchange.ubc.ca
Website: <www.ubcbotanicalgarden.org>
The UBC Botanical Garden usually hosts the
NPSBC's annual native plant sale. This garden has
also been the location for the filming of the television
program, *Canadian Gardener*, hosted by David
Tarrant and produced by the Canadian Broadcasting
Corporation.

Books/Publications/Magazines

Create an Oasis with Greywater, by Art Ludwig. Oasis
Design, 2000

Drip Irrigation for Every Landscape and All Climates,
by Robert Kourik. Metamorphic Press, 1992

Gray Water Use in the Landscape, by Robert Kourik.
Metamorphic Press, 1988

Grow Wild! Native Plant Gardening in Canada, by
Lorraine Johnson. Random House, 1998

*Native Plants in the Coastal Garden: A Guide for
Gardeners in British Columbia and the Pacific
Northwest*, by April Pettinger. Whitecap Books, 1996

*Water: A Practical Guide to Using and Conserving
Water in the Garden*, by Susan McClure. Workman
Publishing, 2000

*Water-Wise Vegetables for the Maritime Northwest
Gardener*, by Steve Solomon. Sasquatch Books, 1993

Videos/CDs

The Rainwater Harvesting CD. The information has been collected from all over the world, from south and north, and from rural and urban areas. The emphasis is on domestic use of rain water harvesting. <www.margraf-verlag.de/shop/infos/1384.htm>

Websites

B.C. Center for Disease Control. <www.bccdc.org>

Health Canada. <www.hc-sc.gc.ca>

U.S. Center for Disease Control. <www.cdc.gov>

Naturescape British Columbia. <www.hctf.ca/nature.htm>

Paving Our Way to Water Shortages. <www.american-rivers.org/landuse/sprawldroughtreport.htm> This site contains the text of a booklet prepared by American Rivers, the Natural Resources Defense Council, and Smart Growth America, 2002

Rain Barrel Information. <www.cityfarmer.org/rain-barrel72.html#barrel> Buckets of links here. And more on the city of Vancouver's rain barrel page: <www.city.vancouver.bc.ca/engsvcs/watersewers/water/conservation/rainbarrel.htm>

Rain Pail. <www.rainpail.com> This company has the marketing rights in Canada and the U.S. for the rain barrel designed in Vancouver, B.C.

Some Seattle ecological landscaping projects:

Cascade Adopt a Park. <www.caup.washington.edu/HTML/LARCH/academics_research/courses/dbprojects5.php>

Broadview Superblock.
<www.seattlepi.nwsource.com/local/95881_model2
0.shtml>
<www.seattlepi.nwsource.com/davart/20021120/day
3secondave.pdf>

Garden of Eatin'.
<www.caup.washington.edu/HTML/LARCH/aca-
demics_research/courses/dbprojects4.php>

Growing Vine Street Project.
<www.djc.com/news/ae/1112543.html>
Seattle Daily Journal of Commerce on-line (and
many others — do a google search of GVS —
Seattle).

The Green Lane. <www.ec.gc.ca/envhome.html>
Environment Canada's website.

Vancouver's Country Lane project. <www.city.vancou-
ver.bc.ca/ctyclerk/cclerk/020709/a5.htm> and
<www/cityfarmer.org/lanes.html>

Vancouver Roof Leader Disconnect Program:
<www.city.vancouver.bc.ca/engsvcs/watersewers/sew-
ers/initiatives/roofleaders.htm>

CHAPTER 6

The Scoop On Poop

January 21

A Pot to Pay In

My boss Mike, an excitable type with a tai chi affliction, parades a tour of English as a Second Language (ESL) students through the greenhouse.

"There it is," he says reverently, pointing to the hotline phone. They seem unimpressed, so he shuffles them along to the compost toilet in the garden — Le Shiteau, as we fondly call it. We've contemplated making it a pay toilet — a loonie for number one, a twoonie for a poonie. Sadly, there were no deposits made today.

Shit Happens at a Compost Garden

"Oh shit!"

That's how I answered the phone today. Not "Good morning, Compost Hotline," my usual cheery salutation. No, a breathy, frantic "Oh shit."

I rushed into the silence. "I'm sorry. I just stepped on a bag of worms."

"Well, somehow 'Oh shit' works for a compost garden," the woman caller said wryly. Prophetic words, indeed.

Mike, my excitable boss, burst into the greenhouse office, arms flailing as he spun into high tai chi mode.

"Rats," he said. "The Malaysians will be here any minute."

"You have a problem with the Malaysians?" I asked.

"No, rats have chewed through one of the plastic compost bins," Mike said.

It never fails. Wes, our head gardener, goes on holidays and we administrators go into crisis.

"We'll just steer the tour around that bin," I suggested.

"I'll set the trap now," Mike said. I cringed, my vegetarian sensibilities assaulted.

When the contingent from the Malaysian ministry of agriculture arrived, we were overly eager to please. Mike handled introductions; there were four men in business suits, three women in traditional ankle-length skirts and blouses. Although their English was impeccable, their accents threw Mike into spasmodic gesturing and e-nun-ci-a-ting. Our volunteer, Emy, deftly ushered them to the picnic table. She had cooked up some authentic Malaysian hors d'oeuvres.

"Warm chick peas wrapped in pastry?" Emy asked.

"Are they halal?" asked one of the women.

"Huh?" I said.

"Kosher," she translated, "are they kosher?"

Emy's face fell. Great, half the population of Malaysia is Moslem and we hadn't considered that fact. I stuffed a handful of appetizers in my mouth, for Emy's sake.

"Mmmm delicious," I said. Mike shook his head at me and started imitating a bird. Charades, now?

"Chicken," he mouthed, "she said chicken, not chick peas."

Not kosher, not kosher at all. Let the tour begin.

"This is our most rodent-resistant composter," Mike said pointing to a three-bin wood and wire system near the grape arbor.

"City Farmer pioneered rodent-resistant composting in Canada," I added proudly.

"As long as you're burying the food waste well, the rodents can't smell it and won't be attracted to the bin," Mike continued, opening the lid. "Of course, a rat can chew through cement when properly motivated, so we line the entire bin with half inch (1.25 cm) wire mesh."

An observant guest raised a shapely brow and pointed to the top lip of the bin. There, embedded into the wire mesh was a flattened mouse, its tail dangling over the edge. Wes must have slammed the lid down in a hurry to leave on his holidays.

"Of course, quarter-inch (.63 cm) wire mesh is best for keeping mice out," Mike explained to our perplexed guests.

"Now over here we have our sheet metal bins, also very rodent-resistant," Mike said, twitching as he lifted the lid.

Oh shit. Flies as thick as locusts swarmed our guests. Not since Wes' last holiday have we seen such plague and pestilence.

"I thought you said that if we covered our food waste with soil and a layer of dry fall leaves or straw that we wouldn't get flies," an attentive tour member said, picking flies off his tongue and out of his nose. Fortunately the women were veiled. Mike shrugged and waved his arms wildly.

"Sir, please don't touch that bin," I said. One of the guests had wandered over to a plastic composter, the one with the rat trap. I grabbed a compost aerator and pole-vaulted across three Malaysians and a bean teepee, slamming his fingers in the lid.

"Ouch, shit!" our guest shrieked.

"I'm so sorry, sir, it's just that..."

"Here kitty, kitty."

Phew, one of the women had spotted the garden cat. Boots was poised to pounce. My eyes sped along the garden path in search of his prey. There, atop the picnic table sat a large rat grazing indiscriminately on the un-kosher hors d'oeuvres.

"Oh shit," I sang out.

"Soooo, would a-ny-one like to see the com-post toi-let?" Mike said. And in a flourish of hand signals, he steered our disillusioned guests towards Le Shiteau.

Hot Calls

Compost Menagerie

Q: Can I compost zoo doo?

A: This call came in from an exotic wildlife refuge in Chilliwack, B.C. They have a lot of iguana and snake doo that they wanted to compost. We spoke to Bert Engelmann, former environmental control officer for the North Shore Health Region, and he advised the following. Go ahead and compost the material separately. Many of these reptiles are carnivores so there could be pathogens in their waste. Compost in an area where there is no danger of leaching into ground water. Use the finished product on ornamental areas only.

Take a Gander

Q: Can I add goose manure to my compost bin?

A: We called the Parks Board to see what their thoughts were on goose manure. They suggested it should be treated as poultry manure and would be similar in nitrogen content and therefore a good starter for a compost bin. Then we checked with our intrepid environmental health officer, Bert Engelmann. Bert discouraged the use of goose manure due to the E. coli (*Escherichia coli*) contained in the feces: this is the culprit that pollutes the water and results in beach and lake closures. So even though geese are primarily vegetarians, unless you have a super hot compost, we don't recommend using goose manure.

Parrot Fever

Q: Can I put parrot poo into my compost bin?

A: We called Bert again to start us off on the right talon. Bert warned that parrots can carry a disease called psittacosis or ornithosis, commonly known as parrot fever. It is a *chlamydia*-like virus that is transmitted to humans through inhalation of infected particles from the feces of the bird. Bert felt it was probably not a good idea to put the parrot feces in the compost bin. But on his recommendation, we sought the opinions of a couple more experts.

After speaking to both the B.C. Veterinarians' Medical Association and the Canada Food Inspection Agency (the folks responsible for quarantining plants and animals), here's our recommendation. Unless your vet has absolutely assured you that your parrot (or other exotic bird) is disease-free, do not put their feces in a compost bin. If they are in fine feather, then put it into your compost, but only if your bin reaches 140 degrees Fahrenheit (60° C). Otherwise, incinerate the parrot poo.

Check with your local health department or center for disease control for updates on the above topics.

September 17

Three Amigos and a Compost Toilet

Our Sun-Mar Excel AC/DC was delivered to the garden today. The compost toilet now resides in its new home, a small building made from recycled wood designed by Ross Waddell. The building was constructed by volunteer extraordinaire Don Ellis who taught woodworking in Vancouver schools for 33 years and by his good friend, Wes Barrett, our head gardener. Now that the three amigos have got this thing working, I guess I'm actually going to have to use it.

Deep into Doo Doo

We deal with a lot of crap here at the garden. And I don't mean the usual bull that goes along with any job, I mean actual shit. I've handled everything from tarantula poo to zoo doo. But it wasn't until we started receiving correspondence from space that I realized just how deep into doo doo we'd sunk.

Dear City Farmer, I ran across your website recently and see that you are promoting compost toilets on earth. We're researching the possibility of composting human waste on Mars for use in growing food. (Hmmm, compost toilets in space, could be a whole new frontier.) *I would like to bring our team of scientists in for a tour of your compost garden next week.*

We were used to international guests, but this would be our first experience with aliens. And then we met Paul.

"I need help," he said.

I was in the middle of harvesting a mucky worm bin. "Don't we all. This is worse than changing diapers."

"I know what you mean," he said. "I live on a boat and I've been composting my own, well, waste, in buckets with a little sawdust."

"Hmmm, gives a whole new meaning to poop deck," I said.

"Yeah well, I'm a marine geologist. I can't bear to flush it into the ocean. But things are backing up and I'm turning off all my lady friends."

"Why not get a compost toilet?" I said. "We love ours. Come see."

As we stepped inside Le Shiteau, a pagoda-style outbuilding at the back of the garden, we saw a man hugging the toilet bowl. It was Mike, who with Gandhian servitude irregularly cleans the throne, usually right before honored guests arrive. And of course, the Martians were coming next week.

"Look at her," Mike said, pride in his eyes. "Isn't she a beauty?"

The Sun-Mar Excel AC/DC gleamed in the fall light.

"So do you flush it?" Paul asked.

"No, but what we do do ..."

I glanced at Mike sharply. Far too many do's for my taste.

"It's a waterless unit; you don't need a plumbing hook-up," Mike said. "So you're producing no sewage and you're not crapping in your drinking water," he concluded.

"How much?" asked Paul.

"We saved over 500 flushes in a year, that's around 3,000 gallons (11,250 liters) of water just by using the compost toilet," I said proudly.

"No, how much did the toilet cost?" Paul asked.

"Well, the toilet itself was around $1,500," Mike said, "but the Buddhist Temple here was another story. You're lucky you already have your housing, well, boating."

"Yeah, well, I'm more of a do-do-it yourselfer," Paul said. "I just need to find a way to process it a little faster and increase the temperature to kill off the pathogens."

"Well, you could try the oven, but then, your girlfriends would think you were a crappy cook," I joked.

"Look, read *Humanure* by Joe Jenkins," said Mike, our wizened old toilet cleaner. "It's the Tao of composting human waste."

The following week, the Martians arrived. They were slight, with Mediterranean complexions.

"Buenas dias," they said.

Hmmm, I thought, clever — speaking Spanish will throw off the tabloids.

"Take us to your toilet." The head Martian scientist was translating.

Our leader led the way. "Our staff is toilet trained," said Mike, pointing to the list of rules on the wall. "They mark their deposits on the calendar: an X for liquids and an O for solids, to keep track of the flushes we save. After number two, they must put a cup of wood shavings into the toilet." (Nothing is sacred here.) "And it smells earthy clean," Mike beamed.

One by one the Martians stuck their heads right into the toilet. "Tidy Bowl?" one asked.

"No chemicals," said Mike, "but what we do do …"

I shot him a warning glance.

"This handle turns the interior drum of the compost toilet, to aerate the umm, contents." Mike pulled out the catch tray revealing a small mound of humanure.

"And you grow food in this compost?" they asked.

"Well, no, just flowers, there's still some concern over human pathogens surviving," Mike explained. "We bury it on a test plot over there behind the shrubbery."

The head Martian said, "They've been growing food in human waste for thousands of years in China and there are plans to use it on Mars."

"There's someone I think you guys should meet," I said.

The following week, Paul dropped by again. "Well, I'm off," he said.

"You're going to Mars?"

"No, Barcelona. That's where MELISSA is."

"Melissa? You've met someone?"

"No, MELISSA is the pilot project those Spanish scientists are working on."

"Spanish?" I said.

"Si. It's an acronym: Micro-Ecological Life Support Alternative — a recycling system destined for Mars that will process human waste and use it to grow plants. It's more advanced than anything they've got on Mir or the International Space Station. They've asked me to join their team."

"You mean they weren't Martians?" I said.

"Oh, nice try, you kidder. Yeah and I'm trading my boat in for a spacecraft. Hasta la vista, the senoritas await me!"

You are now exiting the Toilet Zone. Doo doo doo doo, doo doo doo doo.

Hot Calls

CAT CALL

Q: Can I compost clean cat litter?

A: We called a variety of animal supply houses as well as litter manufacturers in Canada and the U.S. to get the answer to this one.

Most cat litters are made from gravel or clay, although some are derived from other substances like newspaper, walnut husks, corn husks, and even wood-based products, which are then pelleted. Most are scented. The following information applies to both conventional formulations and the "scooping" varieties.

First of all, the clay used in litter is a naturally occurring substance, usually bentonite. It absorbs a lot of moisture (and therefore smells) and actually swells up resulting in "puffed-up slime"! So, as we don't want to absorb moisture to this extent in a compost bin, the litter is an undesirable ingredient.

Secondly, the perfume or deodorizing agents neutralize ammonia (smell) in the litter. In fact, the agents are actually designed to coat the liquid or solid waste to keep the bacteria enclosed. As inhibiting bacterial activity runs counter to what we're trying to do in a compost bin, again, the litter would not be recommended.

And thirdly, clay, though it's naturally occurring, is not something we want a lot of in our garden soil — even if the added perfumes or chemicals in the products left no residual effects in the bin.

And of course we all know that soiled kitty litter is a no-no, too, due to the pathogens contained in the feces.

The Doggy Doo Detective

"CURB YOUR DOG!" the sign said sternly.

I yanked the leash and my companion and I came to a dead halt. "Curb your dog from what?" I asked Guinevere, a carefree, six-month-old, flat-coated retriever. She looked as puzzled as I did. "From chewing your travel shampoo bottle? From eating too many expensive lollipops in that cute doggy shop on Madison Avenue?"

I was happily walking my sister-in-law's new dog in New York this past summer when we came across this sign. Well, okay, I figured out it had something to do with forcing your dog to doo in the gutter. Guinevere must have figured it out too, because right then and there, that defiant pup decided to do her business on the grassy boulevard. And I had no bag. Nor did I have a utensil for flicking it curbside. We fled the scene of the crime.

Back in Vancouver, I got an urgent message on the hotline to call my accountant. Oh crap, not an audit, I thought. But fortunately, she had other business on her mind. Margaret is a member of the Vancouver Dog Owners' Association (Vandog) and she'd heard a rumor that dumping dog waste into park garbage cans may soon be prohibited. She asked if I could do a little snooping around the issue and get back to her with my findings. This sounded like a job for the Doggy Doo Detective. I gave the under-cover agent a whistle.

"So, speak! Give me the scoop on doggy doo," I said to this freelance feces fellow.

"Well, as you probably know, excrement of all types is banned from going into the garbage and subsequently the land-fills in the Greater Vancouver Regional District (GVRD) and in fact, in most regions in North America," he said.

Fair enough: I'd heard the exploding-bag stories. A diligent friend always picked up her dog's poop, put it in a plastic bag, and tied it up tightly. One day two garbage men knocked on her door, steaming from head to toe. Apparently, gas builds up inside the bag and when it is fed into the compactor, it explodes and sprays all over the unsuspecting drivers. City officials are also worried the bags may leak out at the transfer station, contaminating the site and the staff. Woof!

"The scoop law was first introduced in 1971 in the Township of Nutley, New Jersey," the Detective continued. "That's where Martha Stewart was born, you know. Since that time, municipal-ities throughout North America have adopted the law. Officially, it's illegal here to throw dog feces in the garbage," he said dog-matically. "It must be flushed down the toilet or buried in an ornamental area of your garden — officially."

"And unofficially?" I asked.

"Okay, well, there is a bit of a wink and a nod to all of this doggy business," the Detective admitted. Ironically, even in the GVRD Parks where it is officially illegal to throw dog waste in garbage cans, there are little signs directing people to bag it and throw it in the park trash cans. In fact, they even have the doggie bag dispensers there.

"So there's no movement to ban dog poo from park garbage cans?" I asked.

"Not since the intermunicipal committee on dogs tabled the issue last year. And to tell you the truth, the staff at the sewage treatment plants are not all that hot on flushing," he said. It seems the "nuggets" (as they're called in the biz) are rock-hard and gum up the whole sewage system. Plants have to be retrofitted at great expense with special masticators to grind the material up.

"Okay, so let's start from scratch. All you do is take a bag with you when you walk Rover, right?" I asked.

"Right, usually owners tie one to their dog's leash, but many off-leash parks have bag dispensers now," said the DDD. And, he told me, if Polly Purebred prefers, you can buy her lemon-scented, biodegradable doggy bags. Then you use the bag like an inside-out mitten to pick up Cocoa's ca-ca and either take it home to flush or bury it.

"But you have to take it out of the bag first," he said.

"You mean some bozos are flushing the doo with the plastic bags?" Well, I'll be dog-goned.

"And what about double bagging it and then putting it into the garbage can?" I asked with a nudge-nudge wink-wink.

"Right, double bagging is unofficially condoned," he said, confirming my suspicions. "If the waste is well wrapped, there won't be any fireworks. Double bagging is the least of our worries. It's the delinquents who are dropping their pet poo into other people's garbage cans that really get my goat," said the super snoop.

I'd seen some of the desperate signs in my neighborhood. *Garbage men will not pick up my garbage if there's dog shit in it, you mongrel!* "Society is going to the dogs," I said and shook my head sadly.

"And that's not all. I've intercepted some irresponsible owners in Pacific Spirit Park here who bring their bag all right and then try to hide it in the bushes once it's full," said a rabid DDD.

"Such skulldoggery!" I exclaimed.

"And don't even get me started on the joggers and cyclists who race ahead of their pets and have no idea what their animal is doing behind them," he barked.

"Down boy!" I commanded.

"Anyhoo, packing it in and packing it out may not be user-friendly, but owners have to take responsibility for their pets. Not to worry, though, I'll track 'em all down, eventually," said the DDD doggedly.

"So, do you actually spy on people?" I asked. "Hide behind garbage cans in dark alleys? Pop out from behind trees? Stake out fire hydrants?"

"Well, someone better be watching," he said. "GVRD Parks have approximately 1.5 million dog visits a year, leaving 1,125,000 pounds (500,000 kilograms) of product behind. This data is based on 10,000 observations and 800 interviews."

"You've been a busy puppy," I said.

"Right! Then I built a mathematical model based on some figures I got from veterinarians," he said. "The mean fecal output is set at 0.77 pounds (0.34 kg) per day per large dog."

"You built a mathematical model?" I exclaimed. Boy, does this doggy take his doo doo seriously.

I was prepared to let large pooping dogs lie, but not so the walking encyclopedia of feces facts. "Did you know that Paris lost its bid to hold the Olympics there a couple summers back, in part because they had too much dog waste on the sidewalks?" my doo doo advisor asked.

Obviously the French don't fuss much over their feces. After all, it's only a "short-term insult to the environment" and usually disappears within a week. After the Olympic Committee turned them down, a local performance artist drew white chalk circles around the offending piles and stuck little French flags in them. There were 30 to 40 flags in one block. Mon Dieu! Perhaps FiFi should be curbed!

"Tell me about the 'curb your dog' law in New York," I asked innocently. "Oh, yes," he said. "In order to combat the growing dog output problem, many communities, like New York, adopted a 'curb law,' requiring owners to have their dogs urinate and defecate in gutters."

"It sounds like it came out of Britain a dog's age ago," I said.

"Yes, a lot of these bylaws and ordinances were created in the 1800s," he said.

I decided to do a little of my own research. In Chicago,

Ordinance 17.1 "prohibits dogs to be permitted to run at large or to commit any nuisance upon any sidewalk, parkway, or public park." ('Commit any nuisance': now there's a handy euphemism.) Seattle passed its Scoop Law back in 1982, but on the city's website, I found an older ordinance (No. 5) concerning dogs which was approved December 23, 1869. Here are a couple of excerpts which caught my eye "…no dog or bitch shall be permitted to run at large …no slut shall be allowed to run at large while in heat, under a penalty of $5 for each offense." Sounds like they need to curb some of the Olde English.

But in some California cities, according to the doo meister, the laws are pawsitively space age. If owners aren't displaying their dog-waste bag, they can be ticketed. Some trendy Californian dogs wear designer pouches on their collars with little windows showing the prerequisite bag.

The poo hound also told me about some other creative solutions out there in dogdom. For example, in the Borough of Enfield in London, England "dog fouling" is reduced by providing red Poop Scoop bins — dedicated containers for disposal of dog poo in parks and open spaces. Park Rangers carry a supply of Poop Scoop bags. In Seattle, a Dog Task Force has recommended dog bathrooms in parks, consisting of pee poles and gravel and septic systems. The problem with septic systems, though, is that people will just throw their plastic garbage bags right into them and only biodegradable or paper bags would break down. In fact, the problem with any dedicated receptacle is that people throw other garbage into the bins, just as we already see in public recycling bins.

"So what's your vision for the future management of doggy doo?" I asked the Doggy Doo Detective.

"Well, I think we should run some pilot tests on a few different systems and see what works best. But at the minimum, I'd like to see dedicated garbage cans like the red bins in England. The waste could then be subsequently treated in the sewer system or sent to the landfill to be composted in a pet-waste-only area. I'd also like to see portable dog toilets set up in the off leash parks," he said.

"Doggy on the spots?" I laughed. "You're yanking, my chain, right?"

"No, I just mean depositories like compost toilets or septic systems where owners can safely dump their doo," he explained.

I called my accountant and gave her a full report. She told me Vandog is planning to prepare a proposal on pet-waste management to take to the Parks Board. She thinks it's important to the public, for dog owners to take ownership. They just need someone to help pay for it and it's unlikely that the capital will come from the Parks Board.

"It would be so much easier if we could just train the dogs to commit a nuisance directly into the toilet," sighed Margaret.

"Yes," I said, "but we'd still have to curb the number one problem."

"The number one problem?" she asked.

"Yeah," I said, "the males would still forget to put the seat back down."

Hot Tips

WHAT TO DO WITH DOGGY DOO?

If you don't want to risk getting caught throwing out your dog waste, just what do you do with doggy do? Here's what the Doggy Doo Detective recommends:

Flush it. Feces from cats or small dogs can be flushed down the toilet. The problem here is if you're scooping the excrement out of the cat litter, the grains can be a bit messy. And then dumping the dog doo out of those plastic bags is no picnic, either.

Bury It. You can bury the pet poo in an ornamental area of your garden. Do not put it in a food garden: pet feces do contain some harmful pathogens and should not be handled, especially by pregnant women. In fact, there are more than 75 different forms of bacteria and viruses contained in animal feces. So if you don't want to end up with roundworm, remember to wash your hands, children.

Digest it. There are doggy digesters on the market that are more septic systems than composters; they are usually available in pet stores. Or try making your own septic system (see instructions below).

Worms Away. There are people using dedicated worm bins to compost doggy or kitty doo. But experts suggest you let the waste break down a bit first (before adding worms) until the temperature cools, so you don't cook your worms. But do not use this end-product on edible crops, either.

Call a pro. And then there are the professional dog-waste removal services. In places where harsh winters are a fact of life, Pet Poo Pickers do a brisk business. Otherwise when that snow melts, lawns turn into poop soup.

Dare to. And then in the weird department, I found a few other waste-management options on the Internet. You could try the dung-eating beetles out of Australia. Or my personal favorite, an innovative product called Crap-away, a dog deterrent-cum-barbecue sauce that will keep your front yard from being used as a dog toilet. Some of the testimonials on the site swear it's also great for deterring cats and opossums, and for keeping dogs from eating your house.

DO-IT-YOURSELF DOG-WASTE COMPOSTER

We found this "do-it-your-selfer" in a newspaper article by Douglas Sagi in *The Vancouver Sun* (June 23, 1990, p. D9). You'll need a spade, plastic basin, a plastic garbage lid or wood plank, and a package of septic starter (available in most supermarkets for Can$ 2 to $3). Choose a well-drained, slightly out of the way place, not too near tree roots which might grow up into your "septic tank." Dig a hole about a foot and a half (45 cm) deep and a foot (30 cm) in diameter. Make sure the hole is large enough so that the plastic basin fits at the bottom. Our head gardener, Sharon Slack, modified this plan by digging a hole about the same depth and then she sank an old garbage can with the bottom cut out into the ground.

Start collecting your doggy doo and drop it into the basin. Sprinkle a couple of packages of the septic tank starter onto the doo along with a quart (a liter) or so of water. Cover the hole with the lid. Within 48 hours, the septic tank starter, which is non-caustic and promotes natural bacterial growth, will start to digest the doo and you can dump in some more on a daily basis. Add a bucket of water a week and a packet of starter once or twice a month. The dog doo liquefies and leaches into the soil. Any remaining "doo" breaks down into "compost." You should only have to collect the finished product every two or three years. (Use only on ornamental flower gardens.) There is no smell even in the warmest weather and the system has the blessing of the Vancouver Health Department.

February 4

Flush Faced

Laura has started totaling all the emissions we make in our compost toilet; we keep track on a calendar posted on the toilet wall. On a particularly slow day she counted up all the number ones and number twos we'd emitted over a ten month period. She discovered that City Farmer staff had saved 341 flushes just by using the compost toilet. If we calculate that each flush uses between 3.5 to 7 gallons (13–26 liters), that means we saved a minimum of 1,182 gallons (4433 liters) and as much as 2,364 gallons (8866 liters). The older the toilet, the more water it uses. Kind of makes you flush with pride, doesn't it?

Contacts & Resources

Groups/Organizations

Sun-Mar U.S.
600 Main Street
Tonawanda, NY 14150-0888
E-mail: <compost@sun-mar.com>
Website: <www.sun-mar.com>

Sun-Mar Canada
5370 South Service Road,
Burlington, ON L7L 5L1
Phone: (905) 332-1314 Fax: (905) 332-1315
In Vancouver, contact Composting Toilets Western:
(604) 533-5207 or (604) 926-3748

Sun-Mar manufactures several models of composting
toilets as well as an indoor home composter (for
information, go to www.homecomposter.com).

Vancouver Dog Owners Association (Vandog)
401-1917 West 4th Ave.
Vancouver, BC V6J 1M7
Website: <www.vandog.ca>

Books/Publications/Magazines

The Composting Toilet System Book, by David Del
Porto and Carol Steinfeld. The Center for Ecological
Prevention, Concord, MA, 1999

*The Humanure Handbook: A Guide to Composting
Human Manure,* by Joseph Jenkins. Second Edition.
Jenkins Publishing, 1999

Websites

Citizens for Off-Leash Areas (COLA).

COLA is a non-profit organization that was formed to obtain and maintain off-leash dog exercise areas in Seattle.

City Farmer.
<www.cityfarmer.org/comptoilet64.html#toilet>
Read all about how our compost toilet at the garden was built. You'll also find a long list of manufacturers and current book titles.

Crap-Away. <www.crap-away.com>
This site is worth a visit just for a laugh.

Doggie Dooley. <www.doggiedooley.com>
For pet-waste disposal products.

<www.compostingtoilet.org>
International compost toileting news.

Serve Our Dog Areas (SODA). <www.soda.org>
SODA has successfully operated an off-leash dog park in Seattle for many years. They also list other dog parks on their site.

CHAPTER 7

Critter Control

July 12

The Wild Kingdom

Squirrels boldly bury their peanuts in every square inch of the garden. I've even picked them out of the scraggly winter hanging baskets. Mike and Joan came by one evening and spied a large hawk in the cherry tree: Boots has a hunting companion now. We have a family of raccoons living behind the garden. The three little ones drink out of the rain barrels. We were worried they would fall in so we sealed off the opening at the top. Now they knock over our watering cans or drink from the birdbaths. That is, if the dogs, cats, squirrels, or birds don't get there first. A snake slithered across my path the other day. It seems we're an entire ecosystem in one tiny city block.

Diary of a Compost Hotline Operator

Early April

The Pestilent Season

I can tell the season at the garden by the type of pest that is infesting my greenhouse office. Oh, you may think it's peachy that I work in a greenhouse, my computer tucked into a worm bin, but it's not. Ants invade my space come spring; wasps buzz my head through the summer; my desk converts to a mouse toilet in the fall; and a leaky roof dampens my spirits all winter long.

Recently I came to work to discover a curtain of tiny, spotted yellow spiders draped under my computer, hanging from my keyboard. Thousands of them. I quickly called Ike, my biological pest pusher, and shrieked, "I need a fix. There's thousands of spiders, thousands, what do I do?"

I know we're an organic garden but I was freaked out enough to pull the trigger on a can of Raid. Don't get me wrong — I like spiders, they eat other bugs, keep the place neat and tidy, but I'd prefer they weren't nesting on my lap.

I was expecting Ike to give me some elaborate concoction — black eye of Susan with a hair of horsetail, perhaps. Instead he said, "Have you got a vacuum cleaner handy?"

Yes, we'd just bought a voracious little machine the other day. "The Shark" can suck up two bowling balls at a time; those teensy weensies would be caviar to this Great White Guzzler. Sure enough, The Shark swallowed the spider curtain in one gulp. I kept my new weapon at my side all day, ready to pick off any strays.

Mid-April

Spring Comes Marching In

If it's springtime, it must be carpenter ant season. For weeks I've been filling little paper trays with Ike's goopy black stuff and setting it in their pathways. Supposedly, the ants eat the sugary treat and take it back to their queen in the nest where they all die happily ever after. It apparently rips up their insides, but I console myself that it's an organic death. I am usually not given to killing things but I'll just take the karma on this one. I alone have faith in this biological solution. My boss, Mike, and the rest of the garden staff think I am feeding the ants.

"They're getting fatter. They're looking healthier than ever," they chided me.

"Natural solutions take time," I defended myself. "Give it time."

Then the other day Ike dropped in for a spot check.

"I'm encouraged," I said. "Not one of those ants has turned into a flying ant."

"Great, that's a sure sign that their life cycle has been interrupted," Ike said. "Keep those trays full."

Mike and his cronies rolled their eyes.

The next day the greenhouse was full of flying ants, divebombing my head as I answered the compost hotline. I reached under my desk and pulled The Shark out of its holster.

Early May

Those Bird-Brained Gardeners

When our former head gardener threatened to retire, we had him killed and stuffed. He now serves as the scarecrow in the garden. Well, okay, so he's not the real Wes: he's a replica full of plastic bags. But he is wearing Wes' old clothes — jeans, a plaid shirt, and shades. His head is made of old pantyhose stuffed with white cotton batting. Children come into the garden just to say hi to old Wes. They know it's Wes, not only because of the striking resemblance, but because his name badge says so: Wes Barrett, Head Gardener. Well, it's a darn good thing we didn't keep Wes on salary because he's not doing his job these days. In fact, we seem to have more birds than ever — taking mud baths in newly planted garden beds, then washing off in the birdbaths. But the birds have taken to picking Wes' brains. We see flocks of them flying down the railway tracks alongside the garden with Wes' white brains billowing from their beaks. Guess we'll have to change his name tag now: Wes Barrett, Headless Gardener.

Mid-May

Caffeine and Coyotes

Sharon, our new head gardener, is a true urban agriculture crusader, tirelessly fighting off errant vermin. We attribute the influx of birds to the garden this year to Sharon. She's added more fruit bushes for them to hide in, birdbaths, and perches. She's a real bird lover — but a cat lover she is not. She is currently at war with Boots, the neighbor's big black and white cat that has been terrorizing this garden since long before Sharon's time.

As her first line of defense, Sharon decided to place blackberry brambles artistically across the garden beds. It looks quite beautiful and garden visitors are always curious about the practice. "Does it work?" they ask right away.

"Not as far as we can tell," I say. I point to the big holes the cat has dug in and around the twigs. "It's kind of a placebo effect: Sharon believes it's working and that's all that matters."

Wes was never as concerned about esthetics as Sharon was. He wouldn't hesitate to lay an unsightly lattice or cumbersome wire-mesh screen over the freshly dug and planted bed. Ugly but effective, Wes' method kept out cats, squirrels, birds, dogs, and overly-inquisitive new gardeners. On occasion, and only to show who was boss, Wes would even give the boot to old Boots. But not our Sharon: she's a gentle soul. Her latest ploy — advice from a Guatemalan connection — is to spread coffee grounds around the beds. With all that caffeine in the air, the hyped up cats can now get the job done much faster.

And then there was the coyote urine episode. My first question was, "How do they get the urine from the coyotes? Are there little coyote outhouses set up in the wild? Or perhaps milking stations?"

Undeterred, Sharon took to soaking rags in the feral liquid and placing them strategically around the garden. It didn't take Boots long to figure out that there were no coyotes in the neighborhood and he was soon back to his old tricks. Shortly after, we noticed a couple of bamboo accordion gates stretched out across the beds. Sharon's esthetic standard had slipped a notch.

I must confess I'm worried about Sharon. She seems a bit battle weary. Just the other day I saw her eyeing my vacuum cleaner. I could almost see the picture in her mind: Big Bad Boots in the belly of The Shark.

Hot Tips

RODENT RESISTANCE

Compost bins can provide food and cozy shelter for rodents. In urban areas it is important that you choose a rodent-resistant bin to insure that the public health standards are maintained. One-quarter inch (.63-cm) or one-half inch (1.25-cm) wire mesh (hardware cloth) of sufficient strength (16–20 gauge) will keep out mice and rats respectively. Generally speaking, cement would be the most rodent-resistant bin material, followed by metal, wood and wire, and finally plastic. But remember, any rat worth its weight can chew even through cement when properly motivated.

If you are building your own bin, any openings should be no larger than one-quarter inch (.63 cm). The base should also be screened and have good drainage. Make sure the lid is secure and can be latched if necessary to keep out raccoons and other animals with nimble fingers. Wood and wire bins should be lined with wire mesh on the sides, bottom, and underside of the lid.

If you have a plastic bin, put a square of wire mesh underneath the bin to prevent rodents from burrowing up. But most importantly, bury your food waste well so the bin doesn't smell. And even after you've done all of the above, and even if you really know what you're doing, even if you work at a compost demonstration garden and are supposed to be setting an example for the community, keep in mind — there's no such thing as rodent-proof!

The Bear Facts

I was on my way up to Bralorne, B.C., and I had bears on my mind. The historic gold-mining village of Bralorne is located in the mountains (where bears live) between Pemberton and

Lillooet, about five bumpy hours from Vancouver. My friend Laurel had talked me into this all-girls weekend even though I was an inexperienced camper with a Kodiak-sized fear of bears. I was gnawing nervously on a banana as she drove. I rolled down the window and threw the peel into the bushes along the side of the road.

"What are you doing?" Marla cried out from the back seat.

"Oh, I was just doing a little composting," I said.

"That's not composting, that's littering."

Bad compost hotline operator. According to Marla, an experienced outdoors person, responsible environmentalists do not litter, food scraps or not.

"I thought a little bunny would nibble it quick-like," I said sheepishly. "Secondly," Laurel chimed in, "we don't feed wild animals or leave food scraps in the woods because we don't want to adversely affect the ecosystem by getting wildlife dependent on domestic food supplies."

"Right, you carry out what you carry in," Marla said. "And finally, by composting the way you did, you could attract wildlife to the side of the road where they could be hit by a car."

Animal killer will not look good on my resume.

Laurel tried to cheer me. I think the sun will shrivel it up and it will decompose and filter back into the ground.

Yeah right. Karmically, I probably deserve to be eaten by a bear now.

I knew better than to feed the bears. In the summer of 1999, a Wildlife Act (Bill #63) was introduced in the B.C. Legislature, making it illegal to feed or purposely attract bears or other dangerous wildlife. Well, us City Farmers didn't want composting to get a bad rap in all this bear business, so we decided to do a little research. Get the bear facts right from the grizzly's mouth, so to speak.

We started with Bert Engelmann, former environmental control officer from the North Shore region, an experienced composter and member of our compost garden network. Carved out of a mountainous rainforest, North Shore cities get their fair share of bear visitations. When I asked Bert for advice on composting in this bear-o-sphere, he stammered out a confession instead.

"A bear just demolished my composter," he said. It was one of the city-subsidized plastic bins. He also had an older, round, galvanized-mesh bin (called the Lorenzo bin) on his property, but the bear left that one alone.

"I'm sure it was the rotting melons I put in," Bert said. Some fruits like melons and apples have a very strong aroma and bears have a very keen sense of smell. That's why it's so important to pick up fallen fruit from the ground.

"I even had the fruit well buried," said a very em-bear-assed Bert.

Surrey District conservation officer, Fred Barnes, confirmed Bert's melon theory.

"Any really aromatic fruit can still attract bears even if it's buried. But if you cover the food waste with lime (garden lime, not limes), they won't touch it. They don't like citrus fruit either." (Okay, so maybe limes would work.)

Both he and Engelmann agreed that the sturdy wood and wire mesh bins would stand up better to a bear; the plastic ones are easily lifted and tossed. I bet a bear could toss a compost hotline operator pretty easily, too, I thought back then.

"The issue isn't composting, it's improper composting," said Barnes. "The compost bins that have attracted bears are usually not well managed. People have often put meat or fish, grease, fat — all the no-no's into the bin. We get maybe one call about bears in a compost bin to about 20 calls for garbage cans and bird feeders, especially the ones stocked with peanut butter and suet," said Barnes. He also cites dishes of pet food left outside and dirty, meat-encrusted barbecues as other bear delicacies.

We talked to Sylvia Dolson next, president of the J.J. Whistler Bear Society.

"We don't discourage composting; we just tell people to keep their compost bins clean and odor free." Indoor worm composting is another alternative that has worked for many people in the Whistler Mountain ski resort area and the option that the Squamish-Lilloet Regional District is promoting.

Experts say that bears are usually only a problem from April through October. Barnes recommends that you hold off putting your bird feeders out until the coast is clear. But apparently, due to the mild winters we've been having recently in the Pacific Northwest, bears are being spotted year round.

"Bears don't have to hibernate," says Barnes. "If it's cold enough, they will head back up into the mountains and sleep, but with winter weather this mild, they are staying in the lower elevations and scrounging around for food."

"There's been a bear around the property the last few days," the caretaker announced when we arrived at the camping site in Bralorne that warm September afternoon. I surveyed the scene: 11 acres (4.4 hectares) of forest and meadows with a tiny creek running through. If I were a bear, I'd want to hang out here, too. I shivered.

"Come on, I'll teach you the bear song while we set up camp," Marla said. "We used to sing it around the fire at Girl Scout camp." But clearly I was no Girl Scout.

I woke up in the middle of the night with a sore back and a full bladder. Apparently I had forgotten to close my valve. On my Therm-A-Rest, that is. The girls called me "Sleeping on Rocks" for the rest of the weekend. Standing in the tall grass (where snakes live) outside my tent, I dropped my fleece pants down around my shaking ankles. I waved my flashlight madly into the pitch black and sang sotto voce. "The other day, I met a bear, out in the woods, away out there..."

Laurel joined in harmonizing from inside the tent! With the help of the bear song, I survived the first night.

After a full day of hiking in bear country, we arrived back at camp. I'd lived to see another meal. Barbecued salmon for the non-vegetarians, corn, a lentil dish, and fresh blueberries for dessert. After dinner, someone got the smart idea to scrape the leftovers into the fire. The smell of salmon permeated the air.

"Oh great," I said. "I won't even use scented shampoo up here and you guys are using salmon as air freshener."

"Come on, it's still light, let's all go for a walk," Laurel said in a thinly-veiled attempt to distract me.

As we walked along the dirt road that led down to the river (where bears fish), Marla explained to me that in native tradition bears are a symbol of courage. Well sure, easy for them: they're big and hairy with teeth that can rip apart compost bins and toss them as easily as a compost hotline operator.

"Look, this is kind of an isolated road, and it's getting dark, and there's the forest right there," I said. "Don't you think we should head back?"

"Let's sing the bear song," said Marla. I was getting quite bored with her refrain. "We'll sing it in rounds," she chirped.

My teeth and knees were chattering again. "I'm too cold to sing," I lied.

"You can be percussion, Sleeping on Rocks," said my wry friend Laurel.

I was almost finished writing up the bear research when Bert Engelmann called me on the hotline with an update.

"The bear came back," he said. "He had unfinished business."

This time he almost trashed the Lorenzo bin. When I asked Bert how he scared the bear away, I discovered he was an old bear dodger from a way back.

"When I was a student at the Bamfield Research Station, the cook used to feed the bears," said Engelmann. "We used to have to run between the cookhouse and the cabins to avoid them."

And did he learn any tricks in those years for scaring bears off?

"Throwing gravel and banging pots and pans is a sure fire bear repellent," said our very own Grizzly Adams.

The latter trick I knew about from my grandfather's stories. He used pots and pans to scare off the bears at our cabin on Beaver Lake in the Okanagan Valley. They were always snooping around the outdoor pantry drawn by the smell of raw meat. I guess there's just no escaping my bear history. The city of Kelowna was accidentally named by my great Uncle August. As the story goes, some native Indians rode into a clearing one day and spotted a hairy creature. They started yelling, "Kel-ow-na, Kel-ow-na," which means grizzly bear. But it was only my uncle, a rather disheveled and unshaven gold-panner who summoned the spirits daily (the alcoholic kind).

Our last night in Bralorne I did a little spirit-summoning myself. I had a dream about a bear — a spirit bear. I was in a forest clearing sitting on a green towel with a Speedo bathing cap in my lap?! I looked up and saw the bear barreling towards me. For some reason I thought the cap was my Great Protector. I tried to put it on. Now you know, at the best of times it's nearly impossible to put a Speedo cap on, let alone when there's a ton of hairy flesh about to pounce on you. Still, I kept trying. As the bear approached, I saw a flash of yellow in its mouth. Then, just as the bear leaped into the air, I heard the voice of Marla in my head.

"Let's sing the bear song, Sleeping on Rocks."

I threw the cap down and started to sing, vox loudo. "The other day, I met a bear, out in the woods, away out there. The other day I met a bear, out in the woods away out there."

And poof, the bear disappeared right over my head, banana peel and all.

Hot Calls

BANDIT PROOFING

Q: How can I stop raccoons from getting into my compost bin?

A: The caller was referring to a plastic Earth Machine model. We called Bert Engelmann — again. We're getting to be quite the pest ourselves. He suggested the caller secure the bin with two bungy cords (attach them to the bottom vents and stretch up and over the lid crosswise). He also said to secure the trap door by drilling holes through it and through the frame of the bin (two holes on both sides) and bolt with galvanized screws.

We reminded the caller to bury the food well so the raccoons can't smell it. Adding some lime to the food waste will also make it less palatable. If the problem persists, consider a more rodent-resistant bin such as the wood and wire model with a locking lid.

The Great Pigeon Rescue

As I walked up the driveway into the garden on a crisp January morning, I don't know what made me look up, but I did. On the roof of our neighbor Bill's house, a pigeon was frantically flapping its wings at a squirrel. Another pigeon circled overhead. Just then the squirrel ran into the bird's nest under the eaves. I stood and watched the drama unfold. As the mother pigeon tried to defend her nest, she became entangled in some netting that Bill had strung across the eaves to keep the pigeons out in the first place. Now she dangled from the roof peak, struggling to free herself, while the father flapped and squawked anxiously overhead. The more the mother pigeon tried to free herself, the more tangled she got. There she hung, 40 feet (12 meters) up, powerless to stop the cheeky squirrel from scurrying in and out of her nest to get his morning eggs McPigeon. It was 8:55 a.m.

I was in no mood to rescue a pigeon. Just that morning, I had tangled with a mother bird on my apartment balcony. A pair of them was nesting under a table beside my miniature lilac and I was having a heck of a time convincing them to move on. They don't call them homing pigeons for nothing. I had tried the usual scare tactics. I bought one of those cheesy plastic owls and sat that on my railing for awhile. I can still hear the pigeons cackling. Then I tried spreading that sticky stuff along my railing, but they just flew right over it. I've tried barricades too, but every time I thwart their attempts, they kick planter dirt all over the place. I stopped short of draping the entire balcony garden in netting. Aside from the awful aesthetics, I'd probably just get all tangled up myself and wind up hanging off my tenth floor balcony, praying for a fireman to come to rescue me.

I had called Wild Birds Unlimited, our local bird store, to get some advice. They told me you have to remove the nest with the eggs at least three times before the birds will give up. Have you ever tried to remove a nest from a mother pigeon? It is not a pleasant task, separating a mother from her children to be. At the moment, she was winning.

I knocked on Bill's door. At least I could tell him about the hanging pigeon and he could deal with it. Then I'd be done with it. Bill was less enthusiastic than I was about rescuing the bird.

"Don't you have a tall ladder or something?" I said.

"Not that tall," he said. And he didn't hold out much hope that anyone would help rescue the bird. It was only a pigeon after all.

"But it will just die up there if we leave it," I tried again.

But Bill, our favorite, longtime neighbor we could always count on, just shrugged. Still, I knew he was an animal lover. At least he loved Boots — Big Bad Boots, as we liked to call him, a cat only its owner could love.

"What if that were Boots up there and no one was willing to rescue him?" I asked. A likely scenario in my opinion; Boots had made a lot of enemies.

"Well, if you can find a ladder," he said weakly.

"I'll make a few calls," I said and headed for the hotline.

I started calling all the rescue places I could think of: the SPCA, Animal Rescue, Wildlife Rescue, and The Orphaned Wildlife Rehabilitation Society (O.W.L.), but no one makes house calls any more. You've got to rescue the bird, then get it to them. And most of them are located in the boonies — so you might save the bird and then have it die en route. I called the fire department. I remembered all those nice news stories of my youth — firemen rescuing cats and other pets from trees and wells. Surely they would help me out. Unfortunately, they don't do animal rescues anymore, but they reassured me that if I needed rescuing, they'd be there.

"Okay, who do we know with a very big ladder?" I asked the rest of the staff. We came up with a few names. I called Super Glass first. They had just replaced the glass in our greenhouse office. And because they were Super Nice guys, they might actually consider a pigeon worth rescuing.

"Sure," Derek, the owner, said. "I'll try to pull one of my guys off a job, but it could take awhile," he said.

"Thank you so much. You're the best chance that bird has right now," I said feverishly. I was a born-again pigeon lover.

As Super Glass wasn't a sure thing, I continued to make calls. I called a couple of arborists, but they weren't willing to help. I called people who started calling other people. In between phone calls, I kept running out of the greenhouse office to check on the bird. By now a crowd had gathered — City Farmer staff, other people from the building, neighbors. Even Bill was out there. It was about an hour and a half since I'd first spotted the bird and she was no longer struggling. I had to do something, fast.

"I've got it!" I said and ran into the greenhouse. I called our friend at the Parks Board, also a super nice guy.

"We'll send a truck over within the hour," said Paul. I decided not to call Super Glass just yet; I would wait and see who showed up first.

The pigeon husband was now pacing back and forth on the roof. Thankfully, the squirrel had left, but I could see another more menacing threat. Boots, the notorious neighborhood bully, was eyeing the scene. Boots eats or beats everything in sight — mice, rats, birds, other cats. He even makes visitors think twice about coming into *his* garden. That conniving scoundrel wouldn't need a 40-foot (12-meter) ladder, either. I got Sharon to bring out the heavy artillery. She loaded her water gun, her finger twitching over the trigger.

Actually, Sharon is quite the twitcher. No, not the nervous type — a birder. She has a knack for attracting birds. She keeps a list of the ones that visit us tacked to the greenhouse bulletin board: robins, house finches, house sparrows, white-crowned sparrows, common bushtits, Wilson's warblers, hummingbirds, chickadees. We've also had a hawk, woodpeckers, and eagles soaring overhead. Under her careful cultivation, our garden has become a lush oasis in the city for the birds, but anyone can create a wildlife habitat in their back yard, or even on a balcony or patio.

Like us, birds need food, water, and shelter. So Sharon grows flowers, vegetables, and berries that attract our feathered friends, as well as bees and butterflies. And she entices them with all the bamboo perches she provides. Of course, the perches double as bean trellises and tomato stakes. We have several birdbaths around the garden, too, and the blackberry bushes along the fence provide good harborage. Sharon has begun to teach Mike about birds, and twitching seems to come naturally to him.

At 11 a.m., the Parks Board arrived with a cherry picker. I called Super Glass just in time; Derek was about to send a truck over. The netted pigeon was practically motionless now, and her mate was flying overhead. Bob and Dean surveyed the scene and soon had the truck positioned in the driveway. A third Parks guy arrived in a separate vehicle; Jim carried a shoe box with holes in the lid. The driveway was crowded with onlookers now. Apparently it takes a whole village to rescue a pigeon.

Dean would operate the cherry picker; Bob was going to do the rescue. He had birds at home, two cockatoos, so he knew how to handle them. He got into the cherry picker box, armed with heavy-duty clippers and leather gloves. He cooed soothingly to the stressed bird as he rose up to meet her; the bird was limp and eerily quiet. He reached out for her.

"It's still alive," he called down to us.

A cheer went up. He began to cut away at the netting, but the bird was really tangled and it took quite awhile. I heard Bill joke with one of the neighbors that he wouldn't mind if the guy slipped and dropped the bird into the truck's leaf shredder. He was not pleased about those pigeons nesting on his roof. Still, he stayed.

We've had other bird rescues at the garden. One time a baby starling was hopping about the grounds. We rescued the little ball of fluff and Sharon took it to a nearby veterinarian, even though she curses starlings daily in the garden for eating her seedlings. We discovered that we shouldn't have touched the bird. Often in the springtime you find baby birds that appear to be abandoned, but they're actually fledglings who are building their strength by walking around. The parents are usually nearby and the bird does not need rescuing, just guarding from the neighborhood cats.

Then there was the young crow that appeared one day. I'm about as fond of crows as I am of pigeons. Marauding crows have attacked me several times. But this was no marauder; the bird couldn't even fly. It just trailed us like a puppy dog and made a funny caw caw-ghing sound as if it had a cherry pit caught in its throat. He looked up at us adoringly with his ugly little face. Sharon gave him a dish of water and he sat with me at the foot of the greenhouse steps. Then he waddled over and watched the kids' wormshop for awhile. He coughed a bit. He ate some dirt. Drank some more water. And a few hours later, he flew off without explanation. Of course, since that visitation I look at crows differently.

We've had our share of bird tragedies at the garden too. One spring, Wes, our former head gardener, and I set up birdhouses, then anxiously awaited the new tenants. We had checked with the local bird store to find out which birds would nest in our particular houses. We even got fresh new birdseed for our bird feeders (never feed birds old, moldy seed as they can get very ill from the fungal spores). We were ecstatic when we saw a mama and papa sparrow flying in and out of the house atop the grape arbor. Boots was ecstatic, too. We got worried when we saw that he (Boots, not Wes) could stand up, leaning against the back of the birdhouse and reach around to the front of the house with his paw. We shooed Boots away, but then we didn't see the birds for awhile. Wes thought they probably changed nests.

One morning I came in and the birdhouse had fallen to the ground. Inside I found two tiny featherless bodies, already smelling. We'd killed them. Boots had obviously killed the parents, and the babies had starved to death. We had a burial ceremony, then took the houses down. No more helping Mother Nature, we decided then. If we'd done our homework better, we would have known to place the houses up higher and to put wire mesh around them for added protection.

Meanwhile back on the rooftop, the pigeon was finally free. Bob held her firmly in both hands as Dean lowered the cherry picker. Everyone clapped and cheered when Bob alighted. Jim opened the cardboard box; it was lined with a piece of towel. Our Parks Board heroes had thought of everything. Bob placed the trembling bird into the box. We all beamed, even Bill.

Jim jumped in the getaway car and rushed our prize pigeon off to the animal hospital in Stanley Park. Bob went back up in the cherry picker and nailed wire mesh around the former nest site. We didn't want a repeat performance. Jim phoned us just before one p.m. to let us know the hospital had checked out the pigeon and set her free. She flew to a treetop and began preening. They felt she'd make a full recovery!

The next morning the two pigeons were back. They paced back and forth along Bill's roof, trying to figure out how to get back into their nest. Boots watched from his post atop the garden grape arbor. My thoughts flew to my own pair of pigeons still nesting happily on my balcony. During the rescue, I told Dean about the pigeon theme in my life and how I was struggling to get the message.

"Maybe I'm being pigeon-holed in some way. Perhaps I should change careers, become a letter carrier," I said.

"No," he chuckled softly, "Pigeons are doves, symbols of peace and prosperity."

Let's hope they are harbingers then.

Hot Tips

MORE BIRD BUSINESS

There are many things to consider before installing birdhouses: what height to put the nest at, what direction it should face, nesting territories, and more. Different birds have different needs, so make sure you do your research. For example, according to Wendy Morton of Wild Birds Unlimited, chickadee houses should be hung from a height of six to ten feet (1.8–3 m), facing any direction but south. Chickadees have up to three broods per year, so a south-facing nest can be too hot for them in summer.

Both birdhouses and bird feeders have to be placed in locations that don't provide hiding places for cats and other predators. Areas under and around feeders should be kept clean too; otherwise, you can also attract rodents. Rats, raccoons, and even bears love the peanut butter and suet feeders. Compost bins often get blamed for attracting rodents when the culprit is really a messy bird feeder. It's also important to keep the feeders and birdbaths clean to prevent disease. Our longtime volunteer Elizabeth scrubs the birdbaths every week and makes sure there's fresh water in them. Sometimes we have several bird families bathing at once. Occasionally, when we've let the birdbaths run dry, the birds will sit on the edges and stare at us expectantly.

November 7

Mouse Mercy

The mice have moved back in. Ross set up the humane trap for me which Mike says is utterly useless and a complete waste of money.

"All we're doing is catching mice, letting them go, and then they usually beat us back into the greenhouse," he said.

In fact, we have never caught a mouse with it, but that's beside the point.

Contacts and Resources

ANIMALS

Groups/Organizations

B.C. Conservation Foundation
Head Office
#206 - 17564 56A Ave.
Surrey, BC V3S 1G3
Phone: (604) 576-1433 Fax:(604) 576-1482
E-mail: hoffice@bccf.com
Website: <www.bccf.com>

J.J. Whistler Bear Society
Canadian Bear Alliance
204-3300 Ptarmigan Place
Whistler, BC V0N 1B3
Phone/Fax: (604) 905-4209
Website: <www.bearsmart.com>

Books/Publications/Magazines

A New Focus on the Birds of North America, by Kenn Kaufman. Houghton Mifflin, 2000

Bear Smart Kids, by Evelyn Kirkaldy. Jointly produced by the Wilderness Committee and J.J. Whistler Bear Society, November 2002. To order, phone (604) 683-8220 in Vancouver, or toll free at 1-800-661-9453. Or visit the website <www.wildernesscommittee.org>

Websites

Wild Birds Unlimited. <www.wbu.com>
Your back yard bird feeding specialists. They have 290 stores throughout North America and lots of great information for birders.

CHAPTER 8

City Farmer On Tour

May 22

Cities Feeding People

Mike bribed me into speaking with him at a conference in May put on by the International Development Research Center (IDRC). He offered me money, which pretty well always works. The theme was Cities Feeding People: A Growth Industry. On the panel with us were Dr. William Rees (co-author with Mathis Wackernagel of Our Ecological Footprint: Reducing Human Impact on the Earth); Dr. Seydou Niang, a researcher from Senegal; Dr. Anuradha Mittal, policy director for Food First, USA; and Dr. Magda Montes, from the ministry of agriculture in Cuba. The doctors all presented their important research and then we City Farmers got up and did our usual stand-up routine on life at a compost garden. After discussing food problems in third world countries all morning, we all went and stuffed our faces at some posh restaurant.

Cultivating Community in New York City

Your tour begins at the Liz Christy Garden, on the northeast corner of Bowery and Houston Streets on the Lower East Side.

I was reading aloud from the self-guided walking tour we'd been given by the Green Guerrillas, a non-profit group dedicated to turning vacant lots into vibrant community gardens. It was the Green Guerrillas who inspired me to get into urban agriculture. Well, it was actually Andie McDowell in the movie *Green Card* who inspired me, but her character worked with the Green Guerrillas. So needless to say, it was quite a moment when, a decade later, I stepped into their New York offices and shook the hand of a real live Green Guerrilla. I was afraid I might cry as I told my story to executive director, Steve Frillmann. But as usual, it was my partner Barry who burst into tears.

The Green Guerrillas' story is much more moving than mine. It all began in 1973 when Liz Christy, a Lower East Side artist, and a bunch of her friends decided to clean up and beautify a vacant lot on the corner of Bowery and Houston. The enthusiasm of this group of visionaries drew support from the local community and beyond. Nurseries donated plants and materials. Seed companies sent them seeds. Neighbors found objects and turned them into planters and outdoor sculptures. Supermarkets provided vegetable clippings for the compost bins. And dozens of people from all walks of life — artists, architects, teachers, and students from diverse ethnic backgrounds volunteered their time and talents. Out of this one vibrant community garden grew the modern community gardening movement in New York City, a network of more than 700 grassroots groups.

"Where other people see vacant lots, the Green Guerrillas see community gardens," said Steve.

Walk north along the Bowery and take a right on 2nd Street past Albert's Garden. This small site features a pond and some fine shade gardens.

"Don't look up at the buildings!" Barry admonished me. "Are you trying to look like a tourist?"

"I am a tourist," I said.

We were in New York City in the middle of the August 2001 heat wave. Even the air conditioners were sweating, dripping down onto us from high rise building windows. Thanks to Barry, a former New York native, I learned a few rules while I was there, tips that help you blend in. Don't carry your camera around your neck; fold your newspaper in quarters lengthwise on the train; do not under any circumstances pull out your Rough Guide to New York in public.

Continue east to Avenue B and turn left. Four blocks uptown is the 6th & B Garden with its many allotment plots, interesting structures, and a performance space. Stop at the corner to check out the bulletin board for local happenings, then pitch a penny into the Buddha's wishing well.

I took time out from our garden touring to meditate with a couple of dozen New Yorkers in a high-rise building on 32nd Street between Park and Madison. Not your usual tourist activity.

"These weekly meetings are an oasis for all of us," said my old friend and group coordinator Hal.

I was reminded of Voltaire's Candide; each of us are cultivating our own gardens in our own way.

Just east of here is 6BC Botanical Garden, which boasts a pond with a waterfall and a cactus collection.

In neighborhoods where the parks aren't safe and the tall grass in abandoned lots hides subversive activities, creating safe harbors is vital. In one of the poorest sections of the Bronx is the A. Badillo Community Rose Garden.

"Before the garden was created, there was no reason for people to come to this part of the neighborhood," said garden president and founder, Irma Badillo. "There were two vacant lots across the street from each other, attracting garbage dumping, drug dealing, and prostitution."

Now gardeners grow roses there alongside apples, plums, pears, and grapes, for themselves and neighbors in need.

"The garden provides a safe haven and a clean environment for children and adults of all ages to spend time and socialize," said Irma.

Continue east to Avenue C. Turn right and walk down to 4th Street where you will turn east again. Between Avenues C and D is Parque de Tranquilidad, a garden sponsored by the Council on the Environment's "Plant-a-Lot," a program started in the mid-70s by Green Guerrillas' founder, Liz Christy.

According to residents of Brownsville, a neighborhood in Eastern Brooklyn, a critical element in their rebirth is the transformation of vacant lots into thriving community gardens where neighbors gather to work, play, and participate in community life. The Brownsville Garden Coalition is now 14 gardens strong. The popular "Over 50" garden features an African hut, more than 25 fruit trees, a duck pond, and a colorful mural created by the local daycare through the Green Guerrillas' Youth Mural Project.

Across the street you will find El Jardin del Paraiso.

There is ample documented evidence of the positive effects that inner city gardening projects have on urban communities. Gardens help people feel more connected to their neighborhood and engender a sense of community. Residents are proud of the gardens and take ownership of them and ultimately of the surrounding area. Once a garden is in place, it is not unusual for community members to take on other neighborhood fix-up projects, giving them a little more control over their environment.

"It may seem ludicrous to propose that guns, drugs, and violence can be effectively countered by the practice of urban horticulture," writes Richard J. Hull, Ph.D., from the University of Rhode Island, in his article "Psychological and Physiological Benefits of Greenspace" in the journal *Golf Course Management*, August 1994. "Although lawns and gardens cannot necessarily correct social ills, it is likely that the changes they evoke in the attitudes and outlook of residents could."

A short side trip to 3rd Street between B and C will take you past Brisas del Caribe Garden (Breezes of the Caribbean) with its small casitas.

A sagging economy and rising fuel prices devastated inner city blocks in the '60s and '70s. When it became uneconomical to maintain older buildings, landlords abandoned them or burned them down for the insurance, leaving vacant lots in the ashes. The city bulldozed many more. But after decades of economic strife, many of these neighborhoods are being revitalized.

"I looked at the vacant lot across the street and thought about my grandmother," said Jose Soto of Rincon Criollo Cultural Center in Melrose. "She lived in Puerto Rico and had some land where she had a *casita* and planted some medicinal herbs. The very first thing I did when I got my plot was to plant *cilantrillo*, the basic seasoning for all Puerto Rican cuisine."

In many of the Latino gardens you find one-story wooden structures called *casitas*, modeled after the simple dwellings that dot the landscape in Puerto Rico. Gardeners take shelter here from the hot sun or the rains, play music and also teach *bomba* and *plena*, traditional Puerto Rican dances.

Walk up to 8th Street between C and D, where you will find Fireman's Memorial Garden, dedicated to Marty Celic who died in the line of duty fighting a fire on the site.

By the end of a 90-degree day, it wasn't just the heat that was getting to us. The sewer smells were wafting up from the bowels of the city and streets were piled high with bags of garbage. Every day, city residents and businesses generate 25,000 tons of trash. Twenty per cent of that waste is organic, all of which can be composted. Fortunately, the New York Department of Sanitation encourages people to compost through the many programs offered by the city's botanical gardens.

Admission was free the day we visited the Brooklyn Botanical Garden (BBG). Families flocked through the gates, hungry for green space. Like the other Botanical gardens in the city, BBG works with community gardens, block associations, and neighborhood groups. Through their GreenBridge Outreach program, they provide technical assistance and other support such as donating plants, seeds, and bulbs. A key component of their community education program is a compost bin distribution and finished compost giveaway; the compost is made from the leaves and Christmas trees collected by the department of sanitation.

I was oo-ing and ah-ing as we made our way along Butterfly and Hummingbird Trail. Far too many flowers for Barry's taste: he ditched me in the Children's Garden when I got a little too excited over a field of Mexican sunflowers. I found him buried in the superb bonsai collection — the only kind of gardening Barry will get his hands dirty for.

A short side trip at this point will take you to the Lower East Side Ecology Center on 7th Street between B and C, where you can get earthworms or compost for your own gardening projects.

"In 1999, the city tried to sell 114 community garden sites at an unrestricted auction, supposedly to convey land to developers to build housing," said Steve Frillmann. Yet according to a study by Brooklyn borough president, Howard Golden, most of the city-owned lots purchased at this type of auction in the past had not been developed. Instead, the lots became dumping grounds or illegal "chop shops" (where stolen cars are stripped down and parts are sold off). Nowadays, instead of planting gardens, most of the Green Guerrillas' work is focused on trying to preserve gardens.

With the help of garden leaders, community garden coalitions, other non-profits, and a few heavy weights like Bette Midler and her New York Restoration Project, the Green Guerrillas managed to save these gardens, but another 450 or so are still endangered.

"There are more than 10,000 vacant lots that could be developed or sold without harming even one tomato plant," said Frillmann. "But city planners and managers only see the lots as squares on a map; they don't distinguish between a vacant lot and an established community garden."

"Our garden is known for its many mature fruit trees," said Hernan Pagan of the People's Garden in Brooklyn. "It's very unusual to have so many fruit-bearing trees in the middle of the city. And many children never taste fruit that is picked directly from a tree." Most of the trees — cherry, mulberry, apple, pear, and plum — were planted in 1981, the year the garden began.

"It takes years of care to begin to bear fruit," said Pagan. "If we lose this garden, we lose almost 20 years of care and nurturing."

Next door is Green Oasis Garden, which is (barely) visible in Spielberg's movie Batteries Not Included. *To keep the garden from clashing with its urban blight theme, the filmmaker surrounded it with a plywood fence. Other movies shot in this area include* Green Card, Alphabet City, The Super, *and* Joe's Apartment.

Historically, community gardens have always been beaten out by real estate. From the first charity gardens in the late 19th century, on through the liberty gardens of WWI, the relief gardens during the Depression years, and the victory gardens of WWII, construction won out over food production as soon as the economy revived, and urban gardens were bulldozed. But while the early community gardens may have had charity at their roots, the modern community gardening movement "is about rebuilding neighborhood community and restoring ecology to the inner city," writes H. Patricia Hynes in her lovely book, *A Patch of Eden: America's Inner-City Gardeners* [Chelsea Green, 1996, p. x]. There is a lot more at stake here than tomatoes.

Community gardens are not just for gardeners; they serve as public gathering places and rich cultural centers. Neighbors celebrate birthdays together, have picnics, barbecues, play basketball and stage plays.

"There's a huge sense of community here. People meet, hang out, sing, and play the guitar," says Don Loggins of the Liz Christy garden. "Shoppers stop by to sit and take a break; school children come by to see the plants and wildlife. We have a pond with turtles and a beehive that produces 80 pounds of honey a year. It's like you're not in the city."

Around the corner at 9th Street and Avenue C are the 9th Street Community Garden and Park and La Plaza Cultural, both known for their majestic willow trees fed by underground streams, a reminder that this area was originally a wetland. Check out the vegetable plots at La Plaza, where volunteers grow food for the soup kitchen at Trinity Lutheran Parish.

At the Pleasant Park Community Garden in East Harlem, a dozen women of Mexican, Puerto Rican, and Dominican descent work side by side to grow their own vegetables. Tomatoes, tomatillos, bell peppers, jalapenos, beans, cilantro, *epazote*, and *papalo* (herbs used in Mexican cooking) dance together in the sunlight. What they don't need for their own families, they donate to their local food bank. Eighty percent of New York's community gardens grow their own food and share their harvest with the needy through soup kitchens and food pantries.

"This is exactly the way community gardeners throughout the city are making a difference in their neighborhoods, using their gardens to provide services that are sorely needed," says Ximena Naranjo, associate director of the Green Guerrillas. "Community gardens can raise the quality of life for low income New Yorkers," she added.

From here, walk up to 10th Street, between B and C to the CHP Environmental Garden. Popular eateries in the area around Tompkins Square park include Life Café (10th Street & Avenue B), Black-Eyed Suzie's (8th Street, west of Avenue A), Angelica Kitchen (12th Street & 2nd Avenue) and Caravan of Dreams (6th Street and 1st Avenue).

One evening we were on our way to the Village to eat at Cafe Figaro where Bob Dylan used to play. As we walked through Washington Square, Barry got all misty eyed, reminiscing.

"This is where it all happened," he said. "The whole anti-war movement. Abbey Hoffman spoke here, and Alan Ginsberg. Everyone congregated here in the 60s." Barry left New York when he was drafted.

It was that same 60s energy that fueled the community gardening movement in the 70s. In Philadelphia, Ernesta Drinker

Ballard, a respected horticulturist, was starting up the Philadelphia Greens. In Boston, black activist Mel King brought forth the Massachusetts Gardening and Farm Act to enable citizens to grow food rent-free on vacant lots. In New York, WBAI, a community-sponsored radio station, helped spread the word for the Green Guerrillas.

"In 1973, I heard Liz Christy on a WBAI program called *Grow Your Own* and was taken with her enthusiasm," said Don Loggins. "I lived in Brooklyn, but I wanted to be part of her project."

In 1978, gardeners and organizers from these seemingly disparate and uncoordinated greening programs across the country came together in Chicago and formed the American Community Gardening Association. Twenty-five years later, this non-profit group still gives technical support to hundreds of community greening projects in urban and rural communities across North America every year.

In June of 1999, gardeners at the Liz Christy community garden got some distressing news. A developer was tearing down an old building next to the garden to build new apartments and stores and was planning to cut a 22-foot pathway through the center of the garden. But gardeners and community members rallied and after intense campaigning, they managed to negotiate a solution with the developer and the city. The city's oldest community garden would remain intact.

"We've always maintained that community gardens and development don't have to cancel each other out," said Steve Frillmann.

At this point you can take side trips to the many gardens on 12th and 13th Streets between Avenues B and D. Look for the 12th Street Children's Garden at Avenue B, which features a garden-inspired mural painted by kids from the neighborhood.

On our last day in the city, Barry let me look up at some tall buildings — from a distance. We hopped on the Staten Island Ferry. As we chugged past the Statue of Liberty, I said a little prayer for the community gardeners, that their rights and freedoms would be upheld. Barry and I stood arm in arm looking back at the famous Manhattan skyline, the twin towers piercing the blue sky.

The final stop on the tour is El Sol Brillante, on 12th Street between A and B. The decorative fence alone is worth the visit.

September 28, 2002

Garden Memorials

There were lots of inspiring community garden stories circulating after September 11th , 2001. Immediately following the tragedy, one group of gardeners near the World Trade Center site harvested vegetables from their community plot and made a big soup to take back to the firefighters. There have been many other moving accounts of community gardeners gathering for memorials and vigils, and other gardeners have found creative ways to keep the memories green.

In Seattle, WA, flowers left at the Seattle Center by over 70,000 people were later collected by gardeners from the P-Patch Community Gardening Program. Sponsored by the city of Seattle through its department of neighborhoods, the P-Patch is one of the strongest community greening programs in the country, with nearly 70 gardens serving approximately 4,000 active gardeners. On a Saturday morning, gardeners and volunteers gathered to compost over one million flowers, mixing them lovingly with straw and leaves to transform them into a steaming symbol of hope and renewal.

A year later, representatives from the P-Patch gardens flew to New York City with Richard Conlin, a member of Seattle's city council, with 1,400 pounds of Peace Flower Compost. Today they presented their gift of love and solidarity to the Liberty Community Garden in Manhattan's Battery Park City. Liberty was the nearest garden to Ground Zero and some of the north section gardens were used as a staging area during rescue and clean-up efforts. Other gardens in that section were annexed recently to make way for a new bridge. This ceremony was in celebration of the opening of 29 new beds for the displaced gardeners. Seattle's compost will mingle with the soil of New York in each of these garden beds.

"May the flowers and other plants grown in this compost by Liberty gardeners become a beacon of national recovery and renewal from the losses we have all experienced," said Richard Conlin.

Perhaps that renewal has already begun. Michael Ableman (author of From the Good Earth: A Celebration of Growing Food Around the World; On Good Land: The Autobiography of an Urban Farm) flew to New York City to present a proposal for the memorial at the former World Trade Center site. He envisions "an urban farm, replete with greenhouses and kitchens and an education center." Ableman believes the farm could provide food and jobs for the needy year round.

"[The farm could] become a model of a local agriculture-based economy that we can look to as the global and military one begins to crumble," said Ableman.

As founder and director of the Center for Urban Agriculture in Santa Barbara, California, he has the experience to turn this vision into reality.

"The gardens could be set up to accept visitors from all over the world as a memorial that demonstrates that we are a people who know how to bring forth life and nourishment from the ashes and rubble of hate and destruction."

P.S. Steve Frillmann e-mailed me on September 18th to tell me some good news. The Attorney General's office just announced that 198 gardens will be preserved! One hundred and fourteen gardens will be subject to a garden review process, including the A. Badillo and Rincon Criollo gardens. The Green Guerrillas are cautiously optimistic that community gardeners will be invited to actively participate in the process. But disappointingly, 38 gardens are designated for immediate development without a public review, among them the "Over 50" garden in Brownsville.

P.P.S. Even Bonsai Barry is busy cultivating his own garden of miniature bamboo.

The People's Plots in Cuba

"You mean I have to garden my way across Cuba?" asked my partner Barry when I told him about the opportunity for a working vacation. Even though City Farmer is a Vancouver-based urban agriculture group, we have a global outreach, thanks to our website. Thousands of people from around the world visit our site (www.cityfarmer.org) daily to read the latest research on urban agriculture and to e-mail us questions. In 2001, our site received over three million hits from 174 different countries. That's how the Cubans found us: we had three groups visit our little demonstration garden last year alone. And that's when I was invited to visit their urban farms.

The guidebooks joke that the revolution has failed in three ways: breakfast, lunch, and dinner — and they aren't kidding. In December 2001, we landed in Varadero, Cuba's Cancun — well, without the spicy food. To make matters worse, we were vegetarians in a country where chicken and pork are king. For the first few days, we survived on small mounds of rice flecked with beans, mixed salads of shredded cabbage and more shredded cabbage, and soapy black bean soup.

"Would you be upset if I ate some fish?" Barry asked after one day of "starvation."

I was shocked. "You're caving already?"

"I'm protein-deprived," he complained.

"So, you're an agnostic vegetarian, then. As long as your stomach is full of tofu, you believe?"

I overcompensated by gobbling gallons of delicious ice cream and drinking the exquisite espresso by the bowl. Barry, disgusted with my display, smoked cigars and mainlined rum.

I had read that Cuba was an utopian model of urban agriculture — but where was the produce? We began to walk the streets and back lanes, searching for clues. There were no grocery stores to be found — a couple of corner stores, but no produce there. At the state grocery store, people receive their monthly rations of beans, rice, coffee, and lard, but where did they buy milk, eggs, cheese, oil, and veggies? There were no farmers' markets and no street-side vendors selling *frutas*. We spotted a few back yard gardens and contemplated a midnight raid.

One night around seven, we arrived at a Chinese restaurant only to find they were closing up shop: they were out of food. Obviously, there was no need for self-sufficiency in this town devoted to the all-inclusive tourist trade. We found out much later that while tourists grazed at four-star smorgs, real Cubans lived and shopped in Santa Maria, the village across the bridge.

We dined at our hotel that night, where we ate the best meal we had in Varadero — spaghetti with a blob of ketchup.

I knew it was time to move on when I caught Barry hungrily eyeing a wiener dog: dachshunds are everywhere in Cuba. "Havana is the center of urban agriculture," I tried to reassure him. "It's got to be better there. We'll leave tomorrow."

Fortunately, it did get better. We found one of the many farmers' vegetable markets (*mercados agropecuarios*) on our first day out in Havana. After farmers sell their quota of produce to the state, they may then sell their excess directly to consumers at these markets.

"Would you look at the size of those papayars!" Barry exclaimed.

We heard tittering all around us. Hmmm, it must be the New York accent.

"Papaya doesn't have an 'r' on the end, dear," I whispered.

We were staying at a *casa particular*, Cuba's answer to the B&B. Our hosts, Angel and Maria, welcomed us with open arms and a feast fit for the gods. Maria was an inspired cook. Every meal was sublime: green plantain soup, yucca laced with garlic, crispy malanga chips (a root vegetable used like potatoes), fried bananas, *boniato* (sweet potato), stuffed bok choy, rice, beans, and real mixed salads with delicate lettuce, peppers, and tomatoes. Desserts were homemade tropical fruit compotes with black market cheese. I searched my rusty Spanish for a word to express our delight.

"Fantastico!" I exclaimed.

She looked a bit surprised. Hmmm, must be my accent.

Historically, Cuba has depended on food imports in order to meet its needs, as 30 percent of the arable land was devoted to sugar cane, its main export crop. The Soviet Union, Cuba's former sugar daddy, bought much of the crop and provided about 80 percent of their imports. With the collapse of the Soviet bloc in 1989 and the ever-tightening U.S. embargo, Cuba was thrust into economic turmoil. The *Special Period in Time of Peace*, as it came to be known, took a heavy toll on food security. By 1991, the country was experiencing a 60 percent decline in food availability and the population was malnourished.

I spent my evenings reading up on the history of agriculture in Cuba while Barry enjoyed his *Special Period in Time of Napping*.

"Cuba has made what is probably the most immediate and far-reaching change-over from chemical-dependent agriculture to low-input, sustainable agriculture," says Medea Benjamin, co-author of *The Greening of Cuba: A National Experiment in Organic Agriculture*. Until Russia pulled out, Cuba was highly dependent on chemical fertilizers and pesticides, part of the bounty provided by the Soviets. Born of necessity, but with admirable creative spirit, the ministry of agriculture set Cuba on a course of alternative, non-chemical, food production. And urban agriculture is the cornerstone of their new national food program.

Havana, the nation's capital and the largest city in the Caribbean with a population of more than two million, was hit hardest by the food shortages. The city became a focal point in the food recovery plan. Large areas of land around Havana were converted from export crops to food crops; vacant land along roadsides was cultivated, and vegetable gardens sprouted on boulevards, highway medians, rooftops, and balconies. Currently, there are an estimated 5,000 "people's plots" being tended by over 26,000 gardeners.

"Some neighborhoods in Havana are producing as much as 30 percent of their own subsistence needs," says Catherine Murphy, author of *Cultivating Havana: Urban Agriculture and Food Security in the Years of Crisis*.

In addition to the government-sanctioned people's plots, organipónicos (high-yield urban-market farms) sprouted up in urban centers around the country, helping to ease food shortages. There are currently 1,800 urban producers in the city of Havana alone. These intensive gardens usually feature modern irrigation systems and sell a variety of vegetables, herbs, and medicinal plants directly to consumers at 20 percent below farmers' market prices. Asociación Cubana Técnicos Agrícolas y Forestales (ACTAF), a national organization, has many such farms in each of Cuba's 14 provinces.

The Havana provincial branch headquarters was the first *organipónico* we visited. We pulled up to a wire-mesh fence at the end of Santa Beatrice Road in Arroyo Naranjo, one of the 15 municipalities in Havana, where we were greeted by Tara McGee, a 24-year-old Canadian woman who was working on a project here for Lifecycles, a Victoria-based environmental group. We had first met Tara at our own garden when she accompanied some Cuban visitors.

A young girl of about ten clutched Tara's hand and refused to have her picture taken, but her shyness soon wore off. Marianella had grown up next door to the farm and knew every plant by name. As we toured around, she scampered ahead, bringing us gifts of sweet, exotic fruits and fragrant herbs and pointing out the tarantula tunnels in the red soil. We ambled through row upon row of raised beds planted with cucumbers, lettuce, beets, radishes, peppers, cabbage, onions, celery, and traditional starchy root crops (*viandas*) like yucca and boniato. Tomatoes are grown in greenhouses wired with modern irrigation and staking systems. Mangoes, bananas, and guavas skirt the edges of the farm.

"Do you grow any papayars here?" Barry asked.

Marianella burst out laughing.

"*Fruta bomba*," Tara explained.

"Pardon me?" Barry looked embarrassed.

"They call it *fruta bomba* here. Papaya is slang for a woman's, um, privates."

"Frootar bum bar sounds worse," Barry said.

"Yes, it certainly does," I said.

Tara's project was to design and create a herbal and medicinal garden. So far, she and her helper Marianella had only managed to clear the land of rocks, glass, and other debris.

Over a lunch of rice, yucca, fresh garden lettuce, and homemade beer, we chatted with farm administrator, Egidio Eugenio Paez Medina.

"We demonstrate that it is possible to grow food without chemicals here. It started out as a necessity, but now we do it because we've proved it works," he said.

ACTAF's mandate is to promote and strengthen urban agriculture. This farm is being groomed primarily as a demonstration and training site for all *organipónico* producers in the city and secondarily, as a production farm. As at most *organipónicos*, the workers here teach organic principles to gardeners in an on-site classroom; they currently provide outreach and training for all of their 2,000 affiliate members in Havana. Training and on-going technical support are also provided by the ministry of agriculture, horticulture clubs, and other urban sustainability groups.

I had read that, in many ways, Cuba has reverted to traditional organic farming methods — mulching, cover cropping (planting legumes as green manures), applying organic fertilizers such as fermented-cane run-off, using manures, worm compost, and compost. But we saw a gap between the written page and the field. Although soil deficiency was a problem, their compost heaps were poorly maintained and did not provide nearly enough finished product to amend their soil properly. They are, however, experimenting with compost tea — a nutrient-rich liquid byproduct of their worm composting system. At the root of their problems is a lack of proper machinery and staff shortages. At this site, they currently have eight workers and need fifteen.

In contrast, a more established *organipónico* we visited (*UBPC Organopónico Vivero Alamar*) had a brand new tractor and 43 workers with nine horticulturists on staff. (Most other urban farms have one or two.) In addition to a salary, the 43 workers on this farm receive 40 pesos' worth of produce a month. As the average monthly wage is about 217 pesos (roughly US $10), the supplemental food is a godsend. But even at this well-maintained garden, standard organic practices like green manuring weren't being used. Market gardeners keep their beds on a 30-day crop rotation and plant year round. They need fast-growing crops like lettuce and other greens in order to keep their sidewalk stalls full and their customers happy.

In between our formal visits to urban agriculture projects, we sampled some of the street food. The doughy pizzas were bland and filling, but the roasted peanuts and popcorn served in twisted cones of paper were tasty treats. One day I bit into a wedge of coconut pie, reminiscent of Chinese coconut buns.

"Fantastico!" I said.

The vendor gave me a very funny look.

"You'd better look that word up. We don't want another papayar on our hands," Barry said.

Urban agriculture is flourishing in Cuba because of strong government initiatives and grassroots support. But both national and international non-governmental organizations (NGOs) have greatly contributed to the success of the movement.

After lunch at our first *organipónico* visit, Egidio pulled out his well-worn copy of the country's constitution, pointing to a marked section.

"I have the right to associate with other groups to ensure the success of this farm. It's my right." Groups currently working at Egidio's farm include Oxfam, Food First, and Lifecycles. "By sharing information and resources, we can consolidate our efforts to initiate projects," he said.

In fact, this cooperative spirit was embedded in the mandates of all the groups we met with. Project funders included the Australian organization, Permaculture International (the Green Team), Latin America's Aguila, and Canadian groups such as the Canadian International Development Agency (CIDA), the International Development Research Center (IDRC), and Evergreen (a school greening group) — all quietly working away in the shadow of the U.S. embargo.

City Farmer is also working behind the international scene. The society plays an active role in the Support Group for Urban Agriculture with such prestigious international members as the United Nations Development Program (UNDP), the Food and Agriculture Organization (FAO), and the World Bank. It is also the Canadian partner for the Resource Center on Urban Agriculture and Forestry (RUAF) based in the Netherlands. City

Farmer's website serves as an information hub, collecting and disseminating information to the network, helping to move urban agriculture onto the world agenda.

"Pssst, do you want to eat at my family's restaurant?" A handsome young man beckoned to us.

We were standing outside a bleak-looking state-run restaurant. "Sure, anything to get out of eating here," I said. We followed him through the narrow streets of Old Havana. When he ducked into a decaying colonial apartment building and dashed up some dark rickety stairs, we hesitated, but only for a moment. We were starving and out of Maria range.

We stepped inside and found a cheery little bistro with a cook who wasn't freaked out by vegetarians. We were in a *paladar*, the only way to eat in Cuba, according to the guidebooks, since most of the accomplished chefs fled to Miami after the revolution. These private restaurant owners mix entrepreneurship with culinary flair and seem to have no problem finding fresh ingredients.

After a delicious meal, I poked my head into the kitchen and said to the cook, "Fantastico!"

He looked horrified. I ran back to the table, reached into my pack and pulled out my phrase book.

"Oh my God," I said, "your mother is a whore."

"What?" said Barry.

"I just told him his mother was a whore."

"You've done wonders for Canada-Cuba relations," Barry said smugly.

When we got back to Vancouver, we went to buy groceries at our local green grocer — and were overwhelmed by the abundance. Our organic box was delivered that week, too, brimming with fresh produce and variety.

Back at work, it seemed frivolous that we were running a campaign on natural lawn care. I had been embarrassed to tell the visiting Cubans that grass was the largest "crop" in Vancouver. In the U.S., lawns occupy more land than any other crop, including wheat and corn: if you pushed them all together, you'd have a lawn the size of Pennsylvania. There are no vast expanses of lawn in Cuba; in fact, there are no parks to speak of, only concrete squares and monuments.

There is a method to our lawn care madness, though. One of the underlying messages is to encourage people to plant alternative ground covers, including food gardens. Mike Levenston, my boss and executive director of City Farmer, is heading up a research project to determine the food-growing potential in our city using Geographic Information Systems (GIS) analysis on the latest aerial photos of a test neighborhood.

"We are trying to set up a model that cities around the world can use to better document the food-growing potential in their metropolitan areas," says Mike.

Of course, we have the luxury of puttering in our gardens and planning for a possible food crisis, while Cuba is fighting for survival. I wish I'd realized that sooner. When the Cuban farmers visited our garden they told us that some of their workers are actually paid in produce. I joked that Mike paid me small potatoes, too. When they invited me to visit I said I would have to save my potatoes. I might as well have said *fantastico*.

So what is the future of urban agriculture in Cuba? Is it only a temporary solution? Will it fade away if the U.S. lifts the embargo, or have the benefits of urban agriculture had a deeper effect on the country? Certainly, the farmers we talked to have a sense of pride in their accomplishment. They have contributed greatly to food accessibility in their city; created employment; provided green space; and brought communities together with a renewed sense of purpose and solidarity. They are passionate about their new revolution and conscious that they are creating a model for the rest of the world.

Now if only they'd put Maria in charge of the cooking schools, they'd be set.

Hot Web Stories

CITY FARMING AROUND THE WORLD

Visit the City Farmer website (www.cityfarmer.org) and you can travel around the world learning about urban agriculture projects. For example, in Greece, an architectural team prepared a green proposal for the Olympic Village in Athens, complete with hydroponic plantations on the roof (www.urbankit.gr/). You'll read about rooftop gardens in St. Petersburg, Russia (cityfarmer.org/russiastp.html#russiastp), pet pigs running through the streets of Dili in East Timor (cityfarmer.org/diliPigs.html#dili), and bee-keeping in New York City (cityfarmer.org/beekeepNY.html and cityfarmer.org/beesNY.html#beesNY). If you want to learn more about life up north, you'll want to read this next story in its entirety.

INUVIK COMMUNITY GREENHOUSE — ARCTIC FOOD GROWING

By Carrie Young

(cityfarmer.org/inuvik.html#inuvik)

Updated September 20, 2002

Inuvik, which means "place of people" in Inuvialuktun, is a town of 3,200 in the upper corner of Canada's Northwest Territories. We enjoy twenty-four hours of sunlight per day from late May to mid-August, then about four weeks of darkness beginning in December. The Inuvik Community Greenhouse is the most northern commercial greenhouse in North America and the largest community greenhouse of its kind on the planet.

The building houses two areas: raised community garden plots on the main floor and a small commercial greenhouse on a second floor. The garden plots are available to Inuvik residents and some are reserved for Elders and other community groups. The commercial greenhouse produces bedding plants (flowers and starter veggie plants) and also a crop of tomatoes and English cucumbers. There are also rooms in the building for storage, office for staff, and a classroom for workshops and gardening classes.

Community gardening is quickly becoming a solution for urban people, who lack space on their own property or gardening experience, to grow their own food on a small scale. This is especially true for residents of Inuvik who, even if they own property, have permafrost and a very short (and unpredictable) growing season to contend with. Growing indoors and in raised planters makes it possible to produce high quality produce in the North. This is important in Inuvik where the variety and quantity of produce available is limited. High transportation costs and great distances result in expensive and often poor quality produce.

Alice's Colony Garden in Holbaek, Denmark

By Alice Dalhoff Jensen

(cityfarmer.org/alice.html#alice)

Posted September 21, 2001

I have today become the proud owner of a community garden lot with a small house on it. The lot is in a small community garden — in Danish we call them Kolonihaver (as in Colony Garden). The land is owned by the town, and most people prefer just having the soil as their veggie/herb patch. The only "building" on the lots are small shacks for tools and garden furniture; a few have very small houses on them. You then pay a nominal annual fee for the "lease" of the land, which includes running water, to the town, plus whatever you pay initially for the house on the land (and you then own the house).

In my case I have ended up with a true jewel. The house is like a very tiny cottage, has a bedroom, dining room with table and chairs, a weenie kitchen with gas cooking-plates, and a sink. No running water inside, but just outside the door. Johnnie on the spot. It's just sooooo cute and the garden is a masterpiece: three small fruit trees, loads of strawberries, raspberries, rhubarbs, a couple of herbs, and five beds soon ready for veggies (major weeding still required).

A Chicken in Every Garage

No one was paying attention to our news release. We had just commissioned a poll by Ipsos-Reid, a marketing research company, to find out how many people were growing food in Vancouver and Toronto. The results were astonishing. In Vancouver, 44 percent of the households are growing food and in

Toronto, 40 percent. That's about two and a half million Canadians producing some of their own food, including vegetables, fruit, berries, nuts, or herbs, on their balcony, in their yard, or at a community garden. But apparently growing food wasn't newsworthy.

A few years ago we ran a Best Food Garden in Vancouver contest which got a lot of media attention. We told reporters we were looking for gardens teeming with fruit, vegetables, nuts, ethnic or exotic foods. We didn't care if it was in a front or back yard, on a rooftop, a balcony, or a boulevard. And we welcomed unusual features like old bathtubs used for water collection or an old Cadillac turned into a compost bin. In the end, it was mostly neighbors nominating neighbors; our gardeners were a modest lot and their stories made good copy. But clearly we needed a gimmick this time. Worms were usually a good media hook, but we'd done worms to death. It was time for something fresh.

"A chicken in every garage," Mike said.

"What?" I said.

He'd been clucking about the lack of media response and his great outlay of cash for the poll. "If I'd said something about having a chicken in every garage in the release, there would have been a feeding frenzy," he said.

"That's it!" I said.

"Huh?" Mike said.

"For our 25th anniversary. We'll launch a campaign to put a chicken in every garage," I said. "Then we'll slide in the stuff about how many people are also growing vegetables."

"But you're a vegetarian," Mike said.

"Laying hens, we'll only push laying hens," I said.

"But it's illegal to keep chickens in the city," said Mike.

"All media attention is good media attention," I countered, my years in advertising swelling to the surface.

Mike is as much of a media hound as I am. City Farmer started out as a newspaper. In the very first issue in August of 1978, he ran a cover story called *Chickens in Soup*. The article is now reprinted on the City Farmer website. It recounts the trials of Mrs. Centenary, a woman on welfare who was in court to try to keep her chickens. The problem? It is unlawful for city dwellers to keep chickens, among other animal nuisances. She battled it out with the city for six months before being given a suspended sentence and put on six months' probation.

In its broader definition, urban agriculture is not only about growing food, but also about raising poultry, fish, and bees. I checked into the whole issue of "restrictive covenants on animals in urban agriculture" and found out some interesting facts. In simpler times, people kept animals for food and extra income. But as urban areas encroached more and more on rural zones, city officials became more concerned about health issues and smelly, noisy nuisances. So what about those gas-spewing leaf blowers and lawn mowers, huh? I'd rather be woken up by a rooster, frankly.

There's neither rhyme nor reason for some of the animal restrictions. In one urban Australian community, residents may keep up to five chickens, with no distinction between hens and roosters. In St. Louis, you may not keep horses or cows but there is no ordinance against keeping chickens, pigs, or goats! In Annapolis, Maryland, there was a neighborhood ruckus over a burro that was being kept in a shed in a back yard. But the owner got off on a technicality. It seems "burro" wasn't on the list of farm animals that violated city code, and so it was deemed a pet, even though it brayed like a rooster every morning, filled the yard with donkey doo, and made the neighborhood smell like a farmyard. Certain uncommon species — like pot-bellied pigs, kangaroos, goats, and reptiles — have also skirted the law and been given pet status.

"People are still trying to figure out how to beat city hall's bylaws," Mike wrote on his website introduction to the chicken story. "If a neighbor complains, health officials are forced to investigate, but most of the time chicken owners are left undisturbed for years." He warns people to check their city bylaws, keep their yards tidy, and offer their neighbors fresh eggs now and then.

Mike also lists some helpful hints from a woman who has kept a chicken in her apartment since 1996. First, never admit your birds are chickens. Pass them off as Prize Winning Australian Malley Fowl, rare show birds worth thousands of dollars. Second, change that cage every day to prevent the swarm of flies that can arouse neighbors' suspicion and ire. And third, walk your chicken in a park or woods where no one goes(!?). Bring her favorite food so you can retrieve her right away.

In Vancouver, it is unlawful for any person to keep horses, cattle, swine, goats, ducks, geese, bees, turkeys, pigeons, or chickens. Nevertheless, we spotted a few chickens hiding out in some of the Best Food Gardens in the city on judging day. And we even saw a few prize show pigeons. At least we think they were show pigeons.

But I digress: back to the meat of the story. The vegetables. Why are people growing so much food? Well, in a survey we did a couple of years ago, gardeners told us they did it as a hobby, or because the tomatoes tasted better. Some folks grew herbs and vegetables from their homeland, produce they couldn't readily find here. And there are those who garden for stress relief, or because their mother did, and their grandfather before her. But personally, I think it's because they're chicken. People are freaked about what's going into their food — from chemical fertilizers, pesticides, and preservatives to hormones and antibiotics. And they're worried about nutritional content and the safety of genetically-modified foods. Am I still a vegetarian if I eat a tomato infused with fish genes?

Those health and nutrition concerns are fueling the burgeoning organic movement, an industry that has been growing by 20 percent annually over the past decade, according to the International Federation of Organic Agriculture Movement (IFOAM). Many of the leaders of this organic food revolution have their roots in British Columbia, with Vancouver leading the country with the fastest growing organic market. In the U.S., where the organic food industry is now worth a cool $4 billion annually, the federal department of agriculture is taking the business seriously: they have just introduced a new seal that tells consumers whether a product has passed strict organic certification tests. B.C. has been certifying organic foods since 1994 but a national certification program is not yet in place in Canada. Many food activists feel that choosing to buy organic is the single most significant environmental action an individual can take today.

Only three generations ago, the majority of people lived and worked on farms and in small rural communities. At present, nearly all people live in cities and their urbanized surroundings with only two per cent of the population in North America growing food for everyone. Urban farms and back yard gardens may seem like small potatoes when it comes to food production for the masses, but their impact on urban ecology and civic health is significant. Like Gandhi's spinning wheel, that all-important symbol of self-rule, growing our own food allows us to take at least some of the responsibility for feeding ourselves back into our own hands. As gardens grow and neighborhoods become greener, we are more nourished on many levels. Let's face it, putting your hands in the dirt is good for the soul.

"Planners must set aside more of our green space for growing food if they are serious about creating truly sustainable urban centers," Mike continues on the website. "Three possible models include community gardens which have small plots, European-style allotment gardens with larger plots and small cabins for overnight stays, and thirdly mini-market gardens for city dwellers who want to try their hand at commercial growing."

And we mustn't forget roofs; we've got a lot of growing space atop those high rises. A greenhouse on every rooftop — sounds like another campaign to me.

City Farmer has been promoting urban agriculture for 25 years now, but we're not the only group spreading the good word about organic food gardening, composting, water conservation, and air quality. Since our compost demonstration garden opened, nine more have sprung up in Greater Vancouver. Dozens of community gardens have popped up around the city, too; there are three right alongside our demonstration garden. City residents are encouraged to adopt a traffic circle or plant up a street bulge. NeighbourGardens in Vancouver matches people who want to garden with people who are willing to loan them their back yard. And the Fruit Tree Project collects fallen fruit from neglected trees around the city and gives it to food banks.

Chefs are also promoting organic and locally grown food. Some even grow their own; the Waterfront Hotel has a rooftop herb garden that caters to its fine restaurant. There are many organic grocery stores as well as year round organic delivery services and seasonal farmers' markets. Out at UBC Farm, caretaker Derek Masselink is trying to get the first urban market garden in the city off the ground. Our city has become a model for urban agriculture. And this is good news!

But the group that has probably inspired me the most in my 12 years at City Farmer is our collection of 26 Best Food Gardeners. Those people who brazenly grow food in the front yards as well as the back. Who rig up elaborate drip irrigation systems and grow squashes out of garbage bags on their carport roof. The gardeners who grow enough tomatoes to keep their families in tomato sauce for the entire year and still have some to spare for the neighbors. And especially, the city farmers who say, "Bylaws be damned. I'm keeping a chicken in my garage."

Hot Web Story

URBAN FARMERS IN NAKURU, KENYA
By Dick W.J. Foeken and Samuel O. Owuor
(cityfarmer.org/nakuru.html#nakuru)
Posted January 10, 2001

The first and, up to now, the most comprehensive study on urban agriculture in Kenya was the one carried out by the Mazingira Institute in 1985 [Lee-Smith et al., 1987; Memon and Lee-Smith, 1993; Lee-Smith and Memon, 1994). The study was carried out in six towns of various sizes (including Nairobi) which were thought to be representative of "urban Kenya" as a whole. The study populations consisted of households from all income categories. It was found that farming is a very common activity among urban households: almost two-thirds grew part of their food; 29 percent of the urban households did so within the boundaries of the town in which they lived (i.e., urban agriculture per se). Almost half of the households kept animals; 17 percent did so within the town boundaries. It was estimated that about 56 million pounds (25 million kg) of crops were produced in Kenya's urban areas in one season and some 1.4 million animals were kept. Most of the agricultural produce — both crops and animals — was meant for subsistence purposes, which is related to the fact that most urban farmers appeared to be women and that most households carrying out urban farming belonged to the lower income categories.

According to the municipal bylaws, farming practices are forbidden within the town's boundaries. The problem for the municipality is that the enforcement capacity is too small; hence, farming in town has become a very common phenomenon. Nowadays, the municipality allows crop cultivation as long as the crop is less than three feet (one meter) high. Although that excludes maize, even this crop can be seen everywhere. Most people cultivate the common food crops, mostly for their own consumption.

(Note: this site is a large download — over 22,000 words)

December 15

Shimmy Farmers

We had our Christmas party last night. Mike and Joan hosted the event at their co-op and did a beautiful job of making it all come together; their daughters Rachel and Jenny were the gracious servers. We kicked off the evening with a salsa lesson.

"They call it salsa because it's a little bit of everything," said Tony, our instructor. "A little cha cha, a touch of tango, a measure of mambo, a sip of samba, and a swig of swing."

City Farmer is a little like salsa that way — all you had to do was look around the room to see the colorful mix of years, experience, and backgrounds. There was the old guard spread out like the compost chorus line: longtime directors, Bob Woodsworth and Sue Fox, the unsung heroes of City Farmer; Wes bobbing and dipping with his wife Barb; and Mike making macho moves on Joan. He tried to slick back his hair, only he has no hair. Sharon and Terry were clutzing through the cumbia and Jan and I were more jiggle than gyrate when it came to the Cuban motion.

"Ouch," I yelped. We were trying our new steps as couples and Barry had just stepped on my toe. He looked more like he was fording a stream than dancing. "I think you have to be Latin to move like that," Barry said.

We found out later that Tony was Iranian!

Then there was the middle generation — Kate, Laura and Isabelle — who came to us when they were in their 20s. Later that evening, Mike and Joan presented Isabelle and Emiliano with roses; they'll be married in Montreal in January. We raised a glass of champagne to them.

"You guys are family to me," said Isabelle.

I looked over at the newcomers. Dear Jonathan, our new grass man and volunteer head arborist, was doing the cucaracha with the twenty somethings. Stephanie and Krista are our two wonderful new worm workers; the other Stephanie is a faithful volunteer who came to us through Hilary, a former staffer and now dentist.

"I really like these City Farmers," Krista whispered to me.

"Yeah, I know what you mean," I said, as we all shimmied our way into the next 25 years. Viva la salsa!

Contacts and Resources

COMMUNITY GARDENING

Groups/Organizations

American Community Gardening Association
1916 Sussex Road
100 N. 20th Street, 5th Floor
Blacksburg, VA 24060
Phone: (540) 552-5550 Fax: (540) 961-1463
Website: <www.communitygarden.org>

Brooklyn Botanic Garden
1000 Washington Ave.
Brooklyn, NY 11225–1099
Phone: (718) 623-7200 Fax: (718) 857-2430
GreenBridge Community Horticulture Program:
(718) 623-7250
E-mail: compost@bbg.org
Website: <www.bbg.org>
There are three other botanical gardens in New York:
The New York Botanical Garden <www.nybg.org>,
the Queens Botanical Garden <www.queensbotani-
cal.org>, and the Staten Island Botanical Garden
<www.sibg.org>.

City of Seattle P-Patch Program
700 3rd Ave., 4th Floor
Seattle, WA 98104
Phone: (206) 684-0264 Fax: (206) 233-5142
E-mail: p-patch.don@seattle.gov
Web: <www.cityofseattle.net/neighborhoods/ppatch/
default.htm>

Green Guerrillas
151 West 30th Street, 10th floor
New York, NY 10001
Phone: (212) 594-2155 Fax: (212) 594-2380

E-mail: ggsnyc@interport.net
Website: <www.greenguerillas.org>

GreenThumb
City of New York/Parks and Recreation
49 Chambers Street, Room 1020
New York, NY 10007
Phone: (212) 788-8070 Fax: (212) 788-8052
Website: <www.greenthumbnyc.org>
Green Thumb is the largest community gardening support agency in the country.

Just Food
307 7th Ave., Suite 1201
New York, NY 10001
Phone: (212) 645-9880
E-mail: info@justfood.org
Website: <www.justfood.org>

Toronto Community Garden Network
c/o FoodShare
238 Queen St. West
Toronto, ON M5V 1Z7
Phone: (416) 392-1668 Fax: (416) 392-6650
E-mail: cgnetwork@foodshare.net
Website: <www.foodshare.net>

Books/Publications/Magazines

A Patch of Eden: America's Inner-City Gardeners, by Patricia H. Hynes. Chelsea Green, 1996.

The Struggle for Eden: Community Gardens in New York by Malve von Hassell. Greenwood, 2002

Videos/CDs

Sweat Equity. [videotape] This documentary focuses on community gardening activism that was occurring throughout the city of Los Angeles during the years following the 1992 civic unrest. Grassroots actions by local leadership and the sweat equity of community people made it possible to reclaim abandoned land to create urban gardens. Order at <metrofarming.com/aboutsweat.shtml>

Websites

City Farmer.
<www.cityfarmer.org/vanccomgard83.html>
City Farmer maintains a comprehensive list of community gardens in the greater Vancouver area.

The New York Restoration Project. <www.nyrp.org>
Of Bette Midler fame.

The Trust for Public Land. <www.tpl.org>
This group usually deals with large land tract purchases throughout the country and has been instrumental in preserving community gardens in New York.

URBAN AGRICULTURE

Groups/Organizations

ACTAF (Asociación Cubana Técnicos Agrícolas y Forestales)
Contact: Lifecycles
International Partnership Program
527 Michigan Street
Victoria, BC V8V 1S1
Phone: (250) 383-5800 Fax: (250) 386-3449
E-mail: international@lifecyclesproject.ca
Website: <www.lifecyclesproject.ca>

City Farmer
318 Homer Street, Suite 801
Vancouver, BC V6B 2V3
Phone: (604) 685-5832 Fax: (604) 685-0431

E-mail: cityfarm@interchange.ubc.ca
Website: <www.cityfarmer.org>

Fundación Antonio Núñez Jiménez de la Naturaleza y
el Hombre
Roberto Sánchez Medina/María Caridad Cruz
Calle 5ta B No. 6611 entre 66 y 70
Municipio Playa,
Ciudad de la Habana, Cuba
Phone: (537) 209-2885 Fax: (537) 204-0438
E-mail: funapro@cubarte.cult.cu

The Center for Urban Agriculture at Fairview Gardens
598 N. Fairview Ave.
Goleta, CA 93117
Mailing address: P.O. Box 396
Goleta, CA 93116
Phone: (805) 967-7369 Fax: (805) 967-0188
E-mail: mail@fairviewgardens.org
Website: <www.fairviewgardens.org>
Find out all about the great work Michael Ableman
and his team are doing at Fairview Gardens. Also
order both his books (*On Good Land: The
Autobiography of an Urban Farm* and *From the Good
Earth: A Celebration of Growing Food Around the
World*) and his video (see below).

UBC Farm
UBC Faculty of Agricultural Sciences
2357 Main Mall
Vancouver, BC V6T 1Z4
Phone: (604) 822-5092 Fax: (604) 822-6839
E-mail: ubcfarm@interchange.ubc.ca
Website: <www.agsci.ubc.ca/ubcfarm>

UBPC Organopónico Vivero Alamar
Norma Romero Castillo/Miguel A. Salcines López
Ave. 160 Esq. Parque Hanoi

Zona 6, Alamar. H. del Este
Ciudad Habana, Cuba
Phone: 65 37 97

Books, Magazines, Publications

Moon Handbooks: Cuba, by Christopher P. Baker. 2nd
Ed. Avalon Travel, 2000.
This is the best guidebook on Cuba I've come
across and contains a lot of information on urban
agriculture.

*Cultivating Havana: Urban Agriculture and Food
Security in the Years of Crisis*, by Catherine Murphy.
Food First Development Report No. 12.
Order from The Institute for Food and Development
Policy (Food First), 398 60th Street, Oakland, CA.
94618 or by phone at (510) 654-4400, or on-line at
<www.foodfirst.org>

*From the Good Earth: A Celebration of Growing Food
Around the World*, by Michael Ableman. Harry N.
Abrams, 1993

On Good Land: The Autobiography of an Urban Farm,
by Michael Ableman.
Chronicle Books, 1998

The City People's Book of Raising Food, by Helga and
William Olkowski. Rodale Press, 1975

*The Greening of Cuba: A National Experiment in
Organic Agriculture*, by Peter Rosset and Medea
Benjamin. Ocean Press, 1994.
Order from The Institute for Food and Development
Policy (Food First), 398 60th Street, Oakland, CA.
94618 or by phone at (510) 654-4400, or on-line at

Videos/CDs

Beyond Organic: The Vision of Fairview Gardens.
[videotape]
A film about Michael Ableman's work at Fairview
Gardens, produced by award-winning PBS film-maker
John de Graaf and narrated by Meryl Streep. Order
directly from their website
<www.fairviewgardens.org> For institutional or business use, please contact the film's distributor, Bullfrog
Films, at <www.bullfrogfilms.com>, or phone (800)
543-3764.

Websites

Cuba, a photo essay of my trip.
<www.cityfarmer.org/CubaSpringPhotos.html>

International Development Research Center (IDRC).
<www.idrc.ca/cfp>
This site has the Cities Feeding People program.

Resource Center for Urban Agriculture (RUAF).
<www.ruaf.org>
This international organization publishes a magazine
called *Urban Agriculture* three times a year; it is also
available on-line.

ORGANIC GARDENING/GARDENING

Groups/Organizations

Canadian Organic Growers (COG)
125 South Knowlesville Road
Knowlesville, NB E7L 1B1
Phone: (506) 375-7383
E-mail: office@cog.ca
Website: <www.cog.ca>
COG is Canada's national membership-based
education and networking organization representing

farmers, gardeners, and consumers in all provinces. Their quarterly journal, *Eco-Farm and Garden*, is Canada's voice for organic food and growing alternatives.

Ecology Action/Common Ground
5798 Ridgewood Road
Willits, CA 95490-9730
Phone: (707) 459-0150
Website: <www.growbiointensive.org>
Common Ground Classes in Palo Alto:
<www.commongroundinpaloalto.org>
Organic gardening guru John Jeavons publishes a newsletter called *Ecology Action* and offers courses out of his organic farm (Common Ground) in Willits, California.

Salt Spring Seeds
Box 444, Ganges P.O.
Salt Spring Island, BC V8K 2W1
Phone: (250) 537-5269 (no phone orders please)
Website: <www.saltspringseeds.com>
Dan Jason has a great whole-foods' cookbook and a wonderful book on garlic, too. Check them out in the catalogue.

Terra Viva Organics
8480 Dayton Court
Richmond, BC V6Y 3H6
Phone: (604) 448-9373 Fax: (604) 448-9374
Toll Free: 1-866-599-BUGS (2847)
E-mail: info@tvorganics.com
Website: <www.tvorganics.com>
Specialists in organic growing. Order fertilizers, pest control products, seeds and more here!

University of British Columbia
Botanical Garden

6804 SW Marine Drive
Vancouver, BC V6T 1Z4
Phone: (604) 822-3928 Fax (604) 822-2016
Information Line (recorded): (604) 822-9666
E-mail: botg@interchange.ubc.ca
Website: <www.ubcbotanicalgarden.org>

Vandusen Botanical Garden
5251 Oak Street
Vancouver, BC V6M 4H1
Phone: (604) 878-9274 Fax: (604) 263-1777
Website: <www.vandusengarden.org>

West Coast Seeds Ltd
39925 – 64th Street, RR #1
Delta, BC V4K 3N2
Phone: (604) 952-8820 Toll Free Fax: (877) 482-8822
E-mail: info@westcoastseeds.com
Website: <www.westcoastseeds.com>
West Coast specializes in seeds for organic growing.
They have a fabulous catalogue bursting with infor-
mation. You can order on-line, too. And they have a
wonderful demonstration farm where they do seed tri-
als, plus a retail store that sells seeds, supplies, and
whole foods.

Books/Magazines/Publications

*Carrots Love Tomatoes: Secrets of Companion Planting
for Successful Gardening*, by Louise Riotte. Garden Way,
1975

*How To Grow More Vegetables Than You Ever Thought
Possible on Less Land Than You Can Imagine*, by John
Jeavons. Rev. ed. Ten Speed Press, 1991

Organic Gardening magazine
For a one year subscription to this magazine, send
$24.96 [in U.S. funds] to OG, 33 E. Minor St.,

Emmaus, PA 18098, or phone 1-800-666-2206 or visit
their website at <www.organicgardening.com>.

The Basic Book of Organic Gardening, Robert Rodale,
ed. Ballantine Books, 1971

Websites

Garden Humor.
<www.home.golden.net/~dhobson/index.html>
To boldly grow where no one has groan before.

Garden Talk. <www.gardentalk.com>
A catalog of fine tools for gardeners.

Garden Web. <www.gardenweb.com/forums/soil>
The Internet's garden community hosts almost 100
different forums, one of which is of particular interest
to us: Soil, Compost, and Mulch.

Johnny's Selected Seeds. <www.johnnyseeds.com>
A garden supply catalogue.

Feeding the Earth

I HAVE A COFFEE ADDICTION. I only drink two cups a day, but I need those two cups. I once tore a friend's place apart looking for the coffee early one morning. I finally found some beans in the freezer. Then I tore into the cupboards again looking for the grinder. I finally found that and brewed myself a pot. I was just sipping my first cup when my friend walked into the kitchen.

"That's decaff you know," she said to me in her well-mannered British accent.

"I should have known to bring my own stash to a tea granny's house!" I said in an ill-mannered tone, and went screaming out to the corner store to get my morning fix before the withdrawal headache set in.

When Barry and I were in Belize and Guatemala in December 2002, the only coffee you could get was instant. I hadn't brought my own supply there, either. Every morning the waitress would plunk down a jar of brown granules in front of me with a cup of hot water.

"Serves you right for drinking that poison in the first place," said my puritan partner.

"But this is Central America, prime coffee growing country, how can this be?" I railed to him.

Meanwhile, he had bought some locally-brewed alcoholic concoction in the back room of a seedy looking little store. Bitters with herbs and spices stuffed into the bottle.

"This is going to keep me healthy," he said as he shot back his daily ounce. "No bugs will dare invade my stomach."

I shook my head and dumped a spoonful of instant poison into my cup.

I talked to some people we met in Belize about the coffee irony.

"Oh yeah, we get all the rejects here. Not just bad coffee, we get the worst fruit too, and just look at this sugar," one fellow said, pointing to a bowl of locally produced, rough, semi-refined sugar on the table.

Most of the cane sugar in Belize is sent out as pulp and then the refined product is sold back to them at prices many locals can't afford. The best fruit is exported and most of the remaining product not suitable for export is juiced for the local population. (The juice is delicious, mind you!) These poor countries have been turned into agricultural back yards for the rich countries. Food for domestic use then has to be imported at inflated prices. The profits go to the middlemen, landowners, and the multinationals — and the poor stay poor.

I figured the coffee situation might improve once we got to Guatemala. And it did, in a way. At least the coffee here was brewed, but it was still the lowest grade. In recent years, the market has been flooded with low-grade, fast-growing, robusta beans — the type snapped up by the big coffee conglomerates. As a result, the small farmer in Guatemala has been wiped out. Desperate to feed their families, farmers turn to more lucrative crops, like coca to supply the cocaine market.

The only Latin American coffee farmers who are weathering the coffee crisis are those who belong to cooperatives. Growers are guaranteed a fair and stable price regardless of market fluctuation because the product is imported directly from them. I vowed from that moment on to buy only fair-traded coffee, even if it's a little more expensive.

The trip to Central America made me want to take a closer look at the politics of food. How were the choices I was making back home in my grocery store affecting a coffee farmer in a mountainous coffee-growing region in Guatemala? Seeing the evidence of economic injustice and corporate colonialism first hand has made me more determined to make choices that help create self-sustaining village economies.

The fair-traded coffee movement is just one of many sustainability initiatives we can link up with in our own back yard that directly support local economies here and afar. Buying organic food, or at least locally-grown produce, is another, as are saving your own seeds or buying only heritage seeds, and choosing not to buy genetically-modified products. When we refuse to support or cooperate with big business agriculture, we loosen the grip they have on our food system. I know it sounds lofty, but I believe that when we make these seemingly small choices, we are doing our part to eliminate the exploitation and greed that are responsible for poverty, violence, and war thousands of miles away. Sure, the worm is a wonderful symbol of the power of one, but oh, the difference one shopper can make!

One country can make a difference, too. Having done without many of the things we North Americans take for granted, Cuba is developing a living model of self-sufficiency based on sustainable agriculture — and the world is watching.

"Everything at the *huerto* is jerry-rigged," writes Jonathan Cook in his article "Revolutionary Plots" in *Orion* magazine [March/April 2003, pp. 62–69]. "Bits and pieces of metal, wood, and stone, old barrels, pipes, and boards have become storage sheds, herb-drying racks, and planters. The improvisation can be seen as a metaphor for the agricultural revolution in Cuba." Not only are they creating a "new paradigm for green agriculture," Cook concludes, but they are also constructing a "truly sustainable society."

At the City Farmer garden, we, too, are trying to demonstrate sustainable living practices, and by publishing our work on our website, to share what we've learned with the world. Fortunately, we don't have to grow our own fruits and vegetables out of necessity as the Cubans do; food gardening is considered a hobby here. Sure, by promoting urban agriculture and encouraging people to look after their own back yards, we are hoping that the world will become a better place. Growing some of our own food, setting up a worm bin on a balcony, and reducing the use of pesticides and chemical fertilizers are all immediate and practical solutions to the environmental crises — the first layer of compost, so to speak. Still, if what we are trying to build is a more compassionate universe, then there are many more layers to add. It's going to take a lot more than just compost to feed the earth.

When we arrived back home, Barry got sick. He went to bed with a high fever and couldn't get up for a week. At first we thought it was a flu. The second week, we thought it might be hepatitis A; neither one of us had been vaccinated before our trip, having decided to take our chances with the disease rather than the vaccine. He finally went in for blood tests. Sure enough, his liver enzyme levels were elevated, indicating the possibility of hepatitis. He went back for more testing. Turns out it was alcohol poisoning. Looks like we'd both learned a lesson on choosing our poisons. Of course, mine is now organic, shade-grown, songbird-friendly, and fair-traded.

ACKNOWLEDGMENTS

THE CITY FARMER GARDEN is my muse and the funny people who pass through its gates inspire me. I want to thank all of them — past, present and newcomers — for making me laugh all these years and for letting me write them into the script. A very special thanks to the head gardeners (who seem to get lampooned the most) — my old and dear friend, Wes Barrett (the man, not the scarecrow), and my new and dear friend, Sharon Slack (and her alter ego Shee-rahn Slick, eco-warrior princess). Also thank you to our talented and dedicated current staff who read through drafts, caught typos, and gave me valuable feedback: Sharon Slack, Isabelle Oppenheim, Laura Plant, Kate Schendel and Jan Kilburn. There were many other good sports who let me use their names and stories — thank you all.

Three wonderful women friends — Katherine Surridge, Pamela Lee, and Kay Meierbachtol — nurtured the book at the seed stage. John Grogan at *Organic Gardening* magazine commissioned an article based on those early writings and started me on my way. In addition to mentoring me, Eve Johnson, former food writer at *The Vancouver Sun*, connected me with Jim Sutherland, then editor for *The Sun's* eclectic "Mix" section, who made a home for me there. Thanks also to the editors at *The Sun* who continued to publish my work after Jim moved on. The media have been very generous in their coverage of City Farmer, too, and I am very grateful to two TV personalities for playing roles in my book: Oga Nwobosi and David Tarrant.

We are fortunate to work with a very progressive, supportive, and innovative team of people at the City of Vancouver. Without the support of city engineers and staff in the departments of solid-waste, water, sewers, streets, and parks, our programs would never get off the ground. The Greater Vancouver

Regional District (GVRD) has also been very supportive of the hotline and has helped tremendously with promotion and publication of educational materials.

It took a whole village to write every chapter in this book. For the inspiration, big thank you's to Jennifer Blecha, Devon Guest (for the bear song), Paul Morrison, Guinevere (the dog), Margaret Newton, and Vandog. For expert technical or scientific advice, I am much obliged to Brian Holl; the folks at Seattle Public Utilities and Seattle Tilth; John Freeman and Ian Marcuse; Eve Johnson; Mary Appelhof; Al Lynch and the North Shore Recycling crew; Paul Henderson; Doug Kilburn; Bert Engelmann; Fred Barnes; Sylvia Dolson; John MacFarlane; Dirk Lewis; Wendy and John Morton; Arzeena Hamir; Michael Dean; Megan Hemphill; Emy Lai; Ursula Dole; and Dave Buchanan. Jeff Smyth and Ross Waddell made enormous contributions to the water program at the garden and I drew heavily on materials they prepared. Other important water-wise consultants were Frank Skelton, Geoff Johnson, and Daniel Winterbottom.

I am indebted to many people in New York. First and foremost to Steve Frillman at the Green Guerrillas, but also to his co-workers, Ximena Naranjo, Rebecca Ferguson, and all the community gardeners who are featured in the article. Many thanks are due to Ellen Kirby and Julie Warsowe at Brooklyn Botanical Garden, the staff at the New York Botanical Garden, and Adam Honigman, a community garden activist and vital member of the American Community Gardening Association. Namaste to my friend Hal Rosenblatt and bless you, Michael Ableman, for your great vision.

A big hug goes to Tara McGee and Jen Pukonen from Lifecycles who delivered us to the heavenly Maria and Angel in Cuba. We are ever so grateful for the hospitality of Egidio Eugenio Paez Medina and all of the staff of *Asociación Cubana Técnicos Agrícolas y Forestales;* Roberto Sánchez, María Caridad, and all the great people at Antonio Núñez Foundation; and Norma Romero Castillo at *UBPC Organipónico,* her co-workers and lovely translator friend.

Many people also helped me with the technical side of getting a book done. Randy Bennett, thank you for the pictures you took! A special thank you to Marg Miekle for lending me her wise agent, Carolyn Swayze, who generously helped me out with some legal issues. And thank you to Melanie Conn, Bob Potegal, Madeline Milian, Carol Flinders, and Ruth Whyte for the valuable last-minute feedback.

My parents have always been great supporters of my creative life, both figuratively and financially. I am in awe of their ability to keep loving us and giving to us kids. My talented and creative brothers, Don and Todd, deserve a lot of credit, too, for supporting and entertaining me. I am also grateful to my spiritual family — my weekly satsang group and my larger satsang at the Blue Mountain Center of Meditation in California — for not letting me slip off the razor's edge. My deepest gratitude goes to my meditation teacher, the late Eknath Easwaran, who gave me the tools and the words to live by.

I consider Mike Levenston family, too. He's also the best boss I've ever had, a dear friend and advisor, and an ardent cheerleader. He published my work on the City Farmer website when no one else would. In addition to writing his inspiring foreword, he helped me in countless ways with this book — most importantly, he kept me laughing. This book is my gift and my thank you to Mike. How proud I am to be part of this society, its wonderful work. and, of course, its dating service.

Barry Luger is my love and my live-in, natural-born editor. He finds all the holes and inconsistencies in my work and pushes me to a higher level. He also lets me steal his funniest lines.

"What would I do without you?" I asked him one day.

"Write badly," he teased.

But you know, in a way, he's right. Since we've been together, we've been editing each other's lives, rubbing off the sharp edges (we have a lot of them). And slowly but surely, we're becoming better, stronger, and more complete stories. If you like this book, Barry is a big part of the reason.

I thank my lucky stars that the *Diary* is in the gentle company and capable hands of Chris and Judith Plant at New Society. My editor, Patricia Ludwick, tended my book like a gardener, cultivating a rich and fruitful process. It is a privilege and a delight to be working with the entire New Society team.

On the Compost Crisis Line. First published in *Organic Gardening* magazine, May/June 2001. Reprinted by permission of OG magazine. Copyright (2002) Rodale, Inc. U.S.A. All rights reserved. For a one-year subscription send $24.96 to OG, 33 E. Minor St., Emmaus, PA 18098, or contact 1-800-666-2206 or their website at www.organicgardening.com.

Worm Power. An edited version of this article was first published in *Alive* magazine, May 2002.

Lust and Love at the Garden Gate. First published in *The Vancouver Sun*, February 10, 2001.

The City Farmer Compost Tea Party. An edited version under the title, "Where Else but Canada Do You Find Yourself Eating a Seder Supper with Chopsticks?", was first published in *The Vancouver Sun*, June 30, 2001 (Canada Day issue).

Midnight in the Garden of City Farmer. First published in *The Globe & Mail*, October 30, 2001.

Confessions of a Lawn Moron. First published in *The Vancouver Sun*, August 25, 2001.

The Christmas Tree Shredding Ceremony. First published in *The Vancouver Sun* under the title "The Last Ritual of Christmas," December 29, 2001.

Shit Happens at a Compost Garden. First published in *The Vancouver Sun*, August 19, 2000.

Diary of a Compost Hotline Operator. First published in *The Vancouver Sun*, May 19, 2001.

INDEX

SPRING GILLARD,
COMPOST HOTLINE OPERATOR

FED UP WITH SELLING HAMBURGERS AND BEER, Spring fled her lucrative copywriting job at a national ad agency and headed back home to the wet coast. Homeless and jobless, she stumbled into the City Farmer Compost Demonstration Garden in Vancouver and never left. She's been working, writing, speaking and teaching there for twelve years now. When she's not answering compost crisis calls or sifting worm poo, she writes articles on urban agriculture and occasionally ventures into other fields. Her articles appear regularly in the *Vancouver Sun* newspaper and on the City Farmer web site (www.cityfarmer.org). She has also been published in the *Globe and Mail*, *Organic Gardening Magazine*, and numerous other community papers and specialty magazines.

Aside from being a compost hotline operator, Spring's other claim to fame is her stint as ball girl for the Western Canada Lottery television show which, of course, has almost nothing to do with what she does now. Spring graduated from the University of Victoria with a major in French and linguistics which, of course, has nothing to do with what she's doing now. She lives in Vancouver with her partner Barry Luger, the artist/philosopher/ leaky condo expert who has a lot to do with what she's doing now.

If you have enjoyed *Diary of a Compost Hotline Operator,*
you might also enjoy other

BOOKS TO BUILD A NEW SOCIETY

Our books provide positive solutions for people who want to
make a difference. We specialize in:

Sustainable Living • Ecological Design and Planning

Natural Building & Appropriate Technology • New Forestry

Environment and Justice • Conscientious Commerce

Progressive Leadership • Resistance and Community • Nonviolence

Educational and Parenting Resources

New Society Publishers

ENVIRONMENTAL BENEFITS STATEMENT

New Society Publishers has chosen to produce this book on New Leaf EcoBook
100, recycled paper made with 100% post consumer waste, processed chlorine
free, and old growth free.

For every 5,000 books printed, New Society saves the following resources:[1]

25	Trees
2,283	Pounds of Solid Waste
2,512	Gallons of Water
3,276	Kilowatt Hours of Electricity
4,150	Pounds of Greenhouse Gases
18	Pounds of HAPs, VOCs, and AOX Combined
6	Cubic Yards of Landfill Space

[1]Environmental benefits are calculated based on research done by the Environmental Defense Fund and
other members of the Paper Task Force who study the environmental impacts of the paper industry.

For more information on this environmental benefits statement, or to inquire about environmentally
friendly papers, please contact New Leaf Paper – info@newleafpaper.com Tel: 888 • 989 • 5323.

For a full list of NSP's titles, please call 1-800-567-6772 or check out our web site at:

www.newsociety.com

NEW SOCIETY PUBLISHERS